Love's Last Gift

Bébhinn Ramsay was born in Dublin but
now lives with her sons in Florianópolis, Brazil.

ARCH – the Alastair Ramsay Charitable Trust –
established in memory of Alastair Ramsay,
supports Child Health Florianópolis, a family
support project based in Brazil.

All royalties from the sale of *Love's Last Gift*
go directly to ARCH.

www.alastairramsay.net

Love's Last Gift

Bébhinn Ramsay

HACHETTE
BOOKS
IRELAND

To protect the privacy of individuals, initials have been used throughout the text.

First published in Ireland in 2012 by
HACHETTE BOOKS IRELAND

1

Cataloguing in Publication Data is available from the British Library.

ISBN 978 1 4447 4311 1

Typeset in AGaramond and Bodini by Bookends Publishing Services.

Printed and bound in Great Britain by
Clays Ltd, St Ives plc

Hachette Books Ireland policy is to use papers that are natural, renewable and
recyclable products and made from wood grown in sustainable forests. The logging
and manufacturing processes are expected to conform to the environmental
regulations of the country of origin.

Hachette Books Ireland
8 Castlecourt Centre
Castleknock
Dublin 15, Ireland
www.hachette.ie

A division of Hachette UK Ltd
338 Euston Road, London NW1 3BH
England

To Alastair Ramsay
– a man excited by little things.

Part I
GRAINS OF SAND

'Do not go gentle into that good night,
... Rage, rage against the dying of the light.'

Dylan Thomas

'Do Not Go Gentle Into That Good Night'

Beautiful family

It is a peaceful Sunday afternoon in April 2007. I am in a sun-bathed bathroom of a country pub, just an hour south of London. The water bubbles over my hands, framed by the white porcelain of the sink. Outside, I hear children's shrieks, followed by rolls of chubby laughter. My whole body smiles; my toes curl up and I sway gently back and forth in contentment.

As I walk out to the pub's terrace, squinting at the low, early afternoon sun, our youngest son, Liam, flings his body at my legs, desperate to escape his daddy's long, tickling fingers. I shelter him with my body, bending double and nestling my head in his hair. Alastair gives a dramatic sigh of frustration and changes direction to run after our three-year-old, Tom, who screams with high-pitched delight, darts under a wooden fence and half-runs, half-rolls down a pea-green, grassy mound. I watch as Alastair jumps the fence and catches him, rolling with him to the end of the hill.

I stand by the fence, one-year-old Liam in my arms, and survey father and son laughing and spitting newly cut grass from their mouths. Behind them stand a couple of wary sheep, nonchalantly chewing their own grass. A woman in her fifties is sitting at a table by the fence, mesmerised by the same idyllic image. She looks up at me and beams, 'Congratulations on your beautiful family.'

Seven years earlier, bright yellow way-marking arrows had led me straight into creating this beautiful family. These way-markers had brought sudden colour to crumbling stone walls throughout the half-deserted villages of northern Spain along the Way of St James, a 1,000-year-old pilgrimage spanning 800 kilometres. I had followed them diligently as I hiked this path as a twenty-three-year-old graduate. I had walked alone and without a map, warding off the odd dog and lecherous farmer with my hand-crafted ash walking stick. After long days of walking through the monotony of the endless dry stretches of orange-brown cornfields and scorched grass, the glimpse of a bright yellow arrow sprayed on a tree or tiled on a blue background on a wooden milestone made my heart soar: I was on the right path.

At the time, the pilgrimage had been a milestone itself between my childhood and adult life. I had lived a happy, uneventful childhood as the seventh child in a family of eight in a middle-class suburb of Dublin. Here I was at twenty-three, with a degree in international business, a fistful of languages at my disposal and the offer of a coveted job and generous starting salary in London. The future glittered before me like the sun dancing playfully on the sea.

I had just spent a year in Peru, volunteering in a residential orthopaedic clinic, and had a couple of months free before I started my job in London. The pilgrimage had been a perfect low-cost adventure that had seduced me from all angles. In Peru, I had found a huge scallop shell on the beach and when I had shown it to a friend from northern Spain, she had told me that it was the symbol of the pilgrimage that, by chance, passed through her tiny village. In the in-flight magazine from Peru to Europe, I had read a four-page article about the pilgrimage and its 1,000-year history and had arrived home to discover my parents had been passionate armchair enthusiasts for years. Always one to lean towards the serendipitous in life, I had jumped at the opportunity life was pointing out to me.

Before starting out on my pilgrimage, I had found a heart-shaped stone and had packed it in my sparse pack, along with one change of clothes, a sleeping bag and a towel. I was dedicating this pilgrimage to love. As I walked, a storm of thoughts about the past and the future had risen up within me before bringing me to a place of presence. After three weeks of daily walking, I had slipped into a sense of joy at every new step. On a misty morning, I had come to an enormous cairn of stones, rising off the top of a mountain with a huge cross at its core. Each stone represented someone's dream or desire. I had scaled the mound carefully and gently placed the heart-shaped rock among them. With all the fervour within me, I said a silent prayer for life to lead me to true love.

It had been in the afterglow of that pilgrimage that I had met Alastair, when I was still viscerally attuned to the signs of St James.

I had been working in London for six months and was trying to get a position on a project helping an international charity. I was told that the man I had to talk to was Alastair Ramsay. I practised his name in the glass lift as it brought me slowly to his office on the fifth floor. I strode out of the lift and entered his room with gusto, determined to get the position on the team. As I walked in, Alastair sat back in his office chair and signalled for me to sit down. He disarmed me immediately with his wit. He made me drop my agenda and truly connect with him. He was thirty-two, casually dressed with the sleeves of his fleece pulled over his hands. He was long: long arms and long legs. His eyes were a soft greeny-grey, framed behind thin glasses. He smiled as he talked animatedly and bit his lower lip as he listened. He seemed in perpetual movement in the chair as he navigated me in conversation from the origin of my name to comparing the merits of ice-skating on the frozen sea versus on a frozen lake.

I knew his background already from the office who's-who database. He was a senior manager and had worked in the company in both London and San Francisco and had done his MBA at Stanford. Afterwards, he had spent a year as CEO of a Peruvian charity and he was one of the main advocates for the company's pro-bono work. An easy, teasing banter was establishing itself between us, and I left his office with a smile lightening my step.

My gusto paid off and we worked together for two months. In retrospect, those two months were a mating dance between us. Soon, I was holding my breath when I logged in to my email inbox to see if there was a message from him. His visits to the team room sent electric sparks through me as I tried hopelessly to concentrate on the whiteboard. I felt drawn to him, it was a pull that unbalanced me. The universe played its conspiratorial part too, leaving us alone to have dinner on a work trip in Washington when another team member didn't turn up. This dinner was the crossing of the Rubicon. As we sat face-to-face in a cosy French restaurant in Adams Morgan, Washington's international district, each view on life that one of us espoused was an echo of the other's truth, and we laughed in unspoken mutual recognition.

On the day we stopped working together, Alastair asked me to go for a coffee. We met in the office foyer in London and he suggested we go for a walk. I noted the suggestion to myself with excited surprise and half-held my breath as we walked. Our conversation and feet meandered to a nearby park, where we sat, silently, on a bench, looking out on the ducks. Our first kiss was to the sound of birds flapping to take flight and my heart soared, unfettered.

Only later did it strike me that the park was called St James's and I learned that Alastair's middle name was James. The way-marking arrows were clear once again and my heart leaped: I was on the right path.

Competition in generosity

By the time of our beautiful family's pub lunch in April 2007, Alastair and I had been married four and a half years. He liked to refer to marriage as a competition in generosity. I put his idealised view of marriage down to the fact that he had never seen his parents argue. His father, Tom, had died when Alastair was five; his mother had never remarried because she said she had never again met a man who lived up to Tom. Using my amateur psychology, I put Alastair's romantic idea of perfect matches and harmonious marriages down to his childhood. He whispered to me often that I was the woman of his dreams and would state knowingly to friends faltering over love-matches that 'when you know, you know and when you don't know, you know'. At weddings, he would squeeze my hand during the vows and I could feel his glow of contentment. When in traffic, he would run the smooth rim of his wedding ring along his smiling lips.

The romantic in him met the romantic in me. My parents celebrated their fortieth wedding anniversary shortly after Alastair and I met. My father was always sickeningly romantic towards my mother, embarrassing the eternal teenager in me. Beneath my veneer of desired alternativeness lay the cornerstone belief that a loving, lifelong marriage was the founding stone of a happy life.

Shortly after we'd started dating, we went on a skiing trip together. We sat with an English couple over dinner and had finished the story of our brief relationship before the starter arrived. After the dinner, we were making our way alone through the empty, clammy halls of the hotel when Alastair turned to me suddenly and pinned me to the wall. I closed my eyes smiling, waiting for the kiss, drunk on the urgent passion of our intense new relationship. His words rather than lips reached for me. 'We need to live more stories together,' he whispered to me desperately. 'I want to live a lifetime of stories with you and I want them now.' He kissed me hard, and I clocked up one more story.

So began the whirlwind. We tucked stories into every nook

and cranny of our lives. We travelled to twenty countries together, with each journey immortalised in the endless tales that Alastair rehashed and built up over the years with friends: tales of cycling around the incomprehensible streets of Beijing or watching the Pope on television giving an outdoor audience to a crowd at the Vatican, as we lay together in a hotel only minutes away. Accounts of melting in the heat of a beach wedding in Mexico or drunken karaoke with friends in Wales. Alastair knew the secret of cementing a relationship, turning the ephemeral memories in our minds into concrete. Within a year of dating, we had moved from London to Rio de Janeiro in Brazil where a continuous conveyor belt of visitors turned our time into more of an extended holiday than everyday life.

When Alastair finally got down on two knees during a trip home to Ireland in January 2002, on a wild and windy day on the jagged cliffs of Slieve League in the northwest of Ireland, it was two years after we had first met and he was already family to me. The sea below us slapped the cliffs as the wind slapped my cheeks that reddened from an equal measure of pleasure and cold. At the bottom of the mountain, we entwined our fingers through the peep-hole of an ancient Celtic marriage standing stone, committing to the eternal entwining of our lives as had been done thousands of years earlier in Celtic Ireland. About us, a field of sheep and endless stone walls graciously witnessed our commitment as the sky watched clouds float by, and we set off laughing to the pub to put the final seal on the engagement with a pint.

We married later that year in a Catholic-Celtic ceremony, followed by a party of Irish céilidh dancing, samba-costumed mayhem and a late-night international singsong. At the end of the night, my friend S hugged me closely and whispered, 'Congratulations on your fairytale.'

Our first son, Tom, was conceived that night, rounding off with perfection the best day of our lives.

If Alastair was romantic about marriage, he was passionate beyond words about fatherhood. Soon after we'd met, I wrote in my diary about his urgency to have children. Once again, I put this down to the death of his father and the fact that he had missed out on a father–son relationship in his own childhood. In 2003 Alastair became complete at Tom's birth. The enormous grin remained solidly on his face for weeks. He simply gushed over his son; this novice father changed nappies and lulled the baby to sleep like a pro.

Soon after Tom took his first steps, we turned our sights to having another child, and Liam joined the fold in August 2005. I was surrounded now by men who loved me and life was a busy, mostly pleasurable ship that we were captaining. Shortly after Liam was born, we had a couple of friends over to dinner. We put their two children to sleep upstairs with Tom and Liam, and Alastair and I sat whispering in the hall.

'Well,' I said, 'this is what a home with four sleeping children feels like.'

Alastair curled me into his arms. 'I like it,' he said wistfully. 'This is the kind of home I like.'

Now, in 2007, Tom is three and Liam is one, and we are hoping to have two more children. I have had two miscarriages but we are hopeful that the next pregnancies will be more successful.

There is one constant source of tension in our relationship, however. We struggle with how to raise our children, to give them enough time and attention, while both continuing with meaningful and rewarding careers.

For the past four years, I have focused on child rearing, while doing my masters and development work mostly part-time. Alastair's sixty-hour weeks make it difficult for me to put any real energy into my own career, or share the children with him during the week. Since having children, my life has changed beyond all recognition and I clamour for more balance.

Often at night, hours after the children have gone to bed, I sit at the kitchen table in our house in Wimbledon, slowly twirling a glass of red wine in my hand and waiting for Alastair to come home from work. Fourteen hours of riding the rollercoaster of our children's joys and shrieking demands, cooking and endlessly, endlessly washing up have taken their toll on me. I feel a familiar simmering frustration, the sense that I am, once again, waiting for my evening to begin; hostage to Alastair's long hours. The beep of a text message stirs me from my chair. I lower the heat on the evening's dinner wearily, and then check the message and confirm that he will be later than planned. The seed of resentment grows within me and, some nights, I pounce on him as he walks tired through the door.

'Sometimes I think it would be easier without you,' I threw at him once, my words like proverbial plates hurled at him. 'Then I would still be doing everything in this family, but I wouldn't be haunted by this bloody resentment.'

I spat the words at him, as he leaned back, away from me, exhausted, against the kitchen counter.

'Hey,' he barked defensively, 'I do lots for this family.'
He turned his back on me and steadied himself against the
counter.

'There are three people in this marriage,' I growled at him.
'Your work is your bloody mistress and there's no space for me.
How many partners at your company are still with their first
wife? How many?'

He turned to me again, looked at the wildness of my eyes
and sighed. He moved towards me and put his arms around
me. Slowly, I unwound into his embrace. 'It won't be like this
forever,' he soothed me. He nestled his face into my hair and
whispered to me, 'I promise, my love, I will help you achieve all
of your life goals.'

In early 2007 feeling that my career was slipping out of reach,
I decided to go back to full-time work with an international
charity. I hired a friendly Slovakian nanny to take care of the
boys. My job involved a campaign that provides education in
conflict-affected countries. I was planning a series of evaluation
workshops in a number of dangerous destinations, including
Haiti, Sudan and the Democratic Republic of the Congo, and I
became excited at the prospect of such a daring trip.

During a recent skiing holiday, however, Alastair's brother-in-
law, a white African born and bred in Zambia, had cut through
my sense of excitement and adventure. Instead of considering me
courageous, he had told me that I was a foolish, naïve woman
who could be kidnapped and murdered in the blink of an eye.
He told me that I should think of the well-being of my own
children. I had shrugged off his comments with a dismissive
laugh, feeling secure in my own control over life. 'The children

will be fine,' I had said defiantly, 'they have Alastair. We've talked about it before and if one of us is going to die, it's going to be me. Alastair grew up without a father and we don't want that for our children.'

After everyone else had gone to bed, Alastair and I had lounged together on a couch in the foyer of the hotel and sealed the agreement over a late-night coffee.

I am happy to be back at work, relieving my pent-up ambition and quietly kicking myself for the years of career advancement I had lost. At the same time, I miss the boys viscerally and I question how long I will be able to keep doing a full-time job.

A couple of months after starting back at work, I am accepted to start a PhD in Social Policy at Oxford University in September and I am toying with the idea of continuing the more manageable mix of child rearing and studying. Alastair is supportive of the idea and is contemplating reducing his working hours later in the year. These plans are all part of our frequent, wine-fuelled couch discussions of creating our 'ideal life'.

Family holiday

In May 2007, Alastair, the boys and I arrive in the US for a two-week holiday based around a reunion of Alastair's friends from his MBA at Stanford. Summer is ripe to blossom. We arrive in San Francisco jetlagged and weary, having survived the impossible task of keeping an active Liam quiet and amused for the twelve-hour trip. We check into a motel – dragging sleepy boys, teddy bears, bottles and nappies through the windowless corridors – sleep for a couple of hours and then stay awake for the rest of the night. Alastair and I lie on a double bed with the children, holding hands and watching B movies on television. Liam, a real mummy's boy, squirms to get in between us and closer to me. 'By the end of this trip,' Alastair sighs, tickling him, 'you will want me as much as you want your mother.'

We open the curtains to discover it is morning. Our bodies are completely out of sync with the time of day. We throw together our bits and pieces and head downstairs. The motel offers a sugar-fired breakfast of Frosties and donuts, served on plastic plates. We are in a disposable world. We check out quickly, get into our rented car and head south down the Californian coast to a seaside house where we will spend the weekend with Alastair's friends. The smooth movement of the car soon rocks the boys and me to sleep. I open my lead-heavy eyes and marvel at Alastair's ability to stay awake. He laughs easily. 'You sleep my love,' he invites, and turns on the radio at a low volume to keep himself awake. As I close my eyes again, I note that there is something in the way he is safely driving his sleeping family that oozes contentment.

At Santa Cruz, south of San Francisco, we stop for lunch by the sea. The pier juts out over the sea like Michelangelo's languid finger of creation. The seals beneath the pier make a whooping sound that the boys imitate between squeals of laughter. The day is warm and the seafront is almost deserted on this midweek afternoon. The boys and I jump up on a bench with the sea as our backdrop and pull funny faces as Alastair takes our picture. We are all tipsy on the delicious excitement of the beginning of a holiday. Alastair puts his arm around my shoulder as we walk, with the boys skipping ahead of us. 'You know,' he says in a slow, happy voice, 'people must look at you and think what a wonderful mother and what lucky kids.' I hug my arms around his body. 'And they're right: you are and they are.'

I laugh and mock-tickle him under his arm. 'Hey, you're part of this too!' I exclaim. At that, each of us takes a child and swings him high in the air.

At a funfair on the pier, Alastair cheekily pulls us on the merry-go-round without paying. I stand between the two boys holding them on their exquisitely ornate horses as they bob up and down and we all swirl around. As the horses come to a stop, I go to pay for the ride at the ticket-booth. Alastair looks at me teasingly. 'Live a little,' he smiles, with a twinkle in his eye. I laugh, change course and run with the boys to spend all our US change on trying to win big teddy bears we do not want. Our efforts are fruitless and soon the boys tug at our trouser legs to move to the next excitement. We buy ice-cream cones and sit on the sandy steps of the boardwalk. A happy silence falls over the whole family, save for the smack of the boys' concentrated licking. Out of the blue, Alastair dabs his cone playfully on my nose. An ice-cream fight ensues amid peels of laughter. There we sit, our family of four, intently licking our cones, the tips of each of our noses covered in vanilla ice-cream, as we look out together on the endless Pacific Ocean.

Back in the car, Alastair and I begin to talk. I have just finished a book that has me thinking about this stage of our relationship. I am thirty-one and Alastair is thirty-nine. We have been together seven years, and married for four and a half. We have had an intense time together, punctuated by intercontinental moves, endless trips, our wedding and the birth of two children and two miscarriages in rapid succession. All the time, Alastair has been working long weeks and I have been trying to hold on to some semblance of a career.

I turn to Alastair as he drives and I say to him in a sigh, 'You know, Al, it feels like the pace of our life together is finally slowing down.'

'Is that a bad thing?' he asks, as he concentrates on the road ahead.

I am quiet for a while, watching as the endless newness slips past through the window. 'I think what happens now is that our relationship stops spreading itself over more and more new experiences. I think now it goes deeper; more vertical than horizontal, if you get what I mean.' I pause to reflect. 'Al, I have the sense that our great life together will only get richer and deeper from now on.' I put my hand over his on the automatic gear stick and we cruise down the west coast of America in contented silence.

We are the first to arrive at the rented house that we will share with Alastair's American friends for the weekend. After exploring the house, we settle into a large double room with a view of the sea. One by one, Alastair's friends arrive and a stream of catching-up, joking and laughter begins. Alastair loves his friends. This American bunch is a smart and fun group of people, well able to laugh at themselves and others and to match Alastair's English sarcasm. Despite the geographical distances, Alastair always makes a big effort to keep up his friendships. 2007 has been a good year for friends and family. His best friend moved back to England from Canada, and Alastair and he were living in the same country for the first time in six years. He was living one-week on, one-week off at our house while he found a home for his family. After an absence of two years, a close friend from the US has been over to the UK twice in the past couple of months – one time bringing with him an unexpected March snow fall and we spent the morning, Alastair having taken time off work, building snowmen and pelting each other and the boys with snowballs in the park opposite our house in Wimbledon. By chance, Alastair had seen many of his family and friends over Easter too, going on the skiing trip for the first time with his sister, her husband and his adored niece and nephews.

This first night with Alastair's friends is a banter-filled evening of catching up and remembering old stories. Alastair has a funny story or shared joke with everyone, which he rehashes and exaggerates each time they meet. Soon, we are all drinking beer and laughing our jetlag away. Alastair proudly tells them I have been accepted to do a PhD in Social Policy at Oxford University and that we have found a real family home there that we are going to buy on our return. His friends ask about his work, and his possible promotion to director of his company (the results of the promotion process are due out at the end of the week). Alastair has been working with the same company for seventeen years and was one of the youngest partners to be elected. He is now being evaluated for the first time for the highly competitive position of director, which is one of the last levels of promotion within the company. 'Well, the good news,' Alastair says tentatively, 'is that nobody has called me yet to prepare me for not getting the promotion, so I might have got it, but we'll only know next week.'

'The even better news,' I interject excitedly, 'is that if he gets the promotion, he is going to go down to three days' work a week, so we can share taking care of the kids and I can concentrate on my PhD.' We are on the brink of making our 'ideal life' a reality.

When dinner is over, we tiptoe into bed to avoid waking our two increasingly cranky young boys, who are sleeping in cots in our bedroom. That night we sleep curled up together in a tired and happy haze, anxious only to shake off the jetlag of the trip.

In the middle of the night, the peace breaks.

Alastair is shaking with fever and his jerking movements leave me half-awake by his side. He gets up and stumbles to the bathroom with vomiting and diarrhoea. Almost sleep-walking, I get up to bring him water and half-heartedly rub his back. My main concern however is that, for God's sake, he does not wake the boys. They need sleep, even more than we do. My body tenses as Liam awakes with a cranky cry, and I lull him to sleep again in our bed. His father lies next to us shivering uncontrollably, though covered in all the blankets on this warm, early summer, west-coast night.

Alastair spends the next day in bed, while the rest of the group heads off to SeaWorld. One-year-old Liam and I stay in the house too, sleeping on the couch and bringing water and soup to Alastair throughout the day. Alastair is a light shade of green but puts his usual happy face on it. Some other friends arrive and he gets up, exchanges a couple of wobbly jokes and heads back to bed. We put his illness down to a stomach bug, maybe food poisoning from the restaurant in Santa Cruz. He had a hamburger and I had a chicken burger, so we put US beef down as the culprit. His friend P, who studied medicine before going into business, echoes our conclusion for the need of lots of rest and lots of liquids. With that, Alastair stays in bed, drifting in and out of sleep all day. There is a toxic smell of illness in the room. I open a window just a crack to let in some fresh air. Alastair is frustrated at being sick. 'Sorry, love,' he says as he slumps against the pillows, 'this is eating into our holiday.'

I share his frustration, but smile at him. 'Just rest now and let it blow over. In a few days' time, we'll be camping with the boys in Yosemite.'

That evening, Alastair complains of a pain in the right side of his chest. Perhaps, we suggest at the dinner table, he has pulled a muscle through vomiting so violently. The evening is decidedly more sober than the night before and I go early to bed. In the beginning of the night, I am up and down for water for Alastair, dragging my half-sleeping body on automatic pilot.

'Thank you, my love, I know you're exhausted,' Alastair croaks as I hand him a glass of water.

I can only muster up the energy to mutter a sleepy, 'I love you, Alastair. Full stop.'

At three in the morning, Alastair's thrashing continues and a mixture of concern and annoyance wakes me up sufficiently to ask him if he is bad enough for us to get a doctor. I wake two of his friends, J and P, and the four of us sit in a circle of armchairs in the living room, bleary-eyed in our pyjamas. We whisper, so as not to wake all the sleeping children. All of our bodies, except

Alastair's, slump tiredly in the armchairs. Alastair cannot sit still and his eyes are wide open. Using his BlackBerry, I try to find a doctor nearby to make a house call. No luck. We are just outside a small town on the west coast, some three hours south of San Francisco, so we decide to go look for a hospital. 'Just to be on the safe-side,' I assure Alastair, as I help him pull on his clothes.

'Ok,' he says, 'but you stay with the boys.'

'No,' I say adamantly, 'the boys will be fine, I'm coming with you.'

I ask P to take care of the boys and J, Alastair and I leave for the hospital. I grab a towel as we are leaving in case Alastair is sick in the car. Outside in the chilly night air, Alastair and I sit in the back of the car and he lays his head on my knee. He is trembling. The night is so dark that I can only see the outline of his face beneath me. He is breathing fast and his eyes are closed. I gently rub his hair, as he wriggles to get comfortable. He coughs into the towel. We pass a rare lamp-light which spotlights the crimson-red stain on the towel.

This red stain shakes me to full alertness. My heart squeezes with the first pang of panic and I breathe deeply, folding the towel so that Alastair cannot see the blood. We get to the local hospital, which is draped in an eerie silence. Alastair is getting more and more distressed as we bustle him into the reception area. The white light of the waiting room makes us stop in our tracks and blink. I scan the room and its empty, standard-issue, white plastic waiting chairs and move towards a half-dozing receptionist, removed from us behind bullet-proof glass. I quickly give Alastair's name and details, reassure her that he has health insurance and relate his symptoms: twenty-four hours of vomiting, diarrhoea and fever with recent pain in the right side of his chest and now coughing up blood.

The mention of blood whirrs the receptionist into action and Alastair is quickly admitted, laid down on a narrow bed in a small, dark room and sedated. As Alastair's body calms, I feel myself calming down too. Reassuring thoughts massage my mind. We are at the hospital. We are in the best place possible for Alastair. I sit in a chair by his bed and hold his hand. I provide information to a trickle of doctors that come in and out of his room. They ask me a series of questions, including his medical history, where he has travelled to lately, his symptoms and his movements over the past few days.

I tell them what I know. He is thirty-nine, in very good health: he had a full medical in November and the results were great. The only risk factors that I could think of were that he has slightly high cholesterol, travelled to a number of countries, including Ghana and Russia, in the past year and that his father had died at the age of forty-three of non-alcoholic liver failure. I rattle off the information in a calm, succinct way. I grab on to these questions and answers as a way to avoid the rising thoughts and emotions of concern coursing through my body. I slap myself into dealing with this one current bite of reality.

As I talk to the doctors, Alastair comes out of sedation and his breathing is laboured. The doctors push his bed down the corridor to a larger, brighter room and hook him up to machines to monitor his oxygen intake. They take an x-ray of his lungs. A doctor holds up the x-ray against the light, which shows that the right side of his lung is almost completely white. 'Pneumonia,' they diagnose. A diagnosis! My attention jumps on it. Like the questions and answers before, the diagnosis is a stepping stone to avoid slipping into the river of emotions and worrying thoughts that is steadily rising within me.

'Well, my love,' I soothe Alastair, 'that explains the pain in your chest.'

Pneumonia, however, appears to be a symptom rather than the cause. The pace of the doctors and nurses increases, their steps are more hurried and their faces more closed as they move in and out of the room.

'We are going to put you on intravenous antibiotics and an oxygen mask to help you breathe more easily,' one of the myriad of doctors explains and whips himself out of the way before we can ask a question.

Minutes later, they suggest putting in a catheter. Alastair removes the oxygen mask. 'Why are you doing that?' he asks, breathless and anxious.

'You're going to be immobilised for some time, until you can breathe more easily, so you won't be able to go to the bathroom,' the doctors inform him. I place the mask gently back over his mouth.

I grab a doctor by the arm as he is leaving the room. 'What's going on?' I half-croak as my voice breaks.

'We don't know,' he replies curtly and removes his arm from my grasp.

I am wobbling on the stepping stones and the river of emotions is gathering force. With effort now, Alastair moves his oxygen mask to the side. 'I am so glad you are here with me,' he wheezes.

I smile at him, trying to appear reassuring. 'Where else would I be?'

Code red

The doctors congregate in the hall outside Alastair's room and I hear a buzz of hushed voices. Suddenly, two doctors come briskly into the room, wielding white disposable face-masks.

'We suspect it is tuberculosis,' the doctors inform me, 'from his recent trip to Russia.'

My face flushes with a sense of panic. 'We have two small boys,' I tell them, 'aged one and three and they were in our bed with us. Are they in danger? Should I ask for them to be brought here?'

'No, no,' they assure me. 'No need to bring them to the hospital until we are sure what we are dealing with.'

Alastair moves to take off his mask, but cannot do it alone, so I bend over him to help. 'Go to the boys,' he whispers in an out-breath.

'No,' I say adamantly, 'I am staying here with you.'

As Alastair slips out of consciousness, I sit by his side, furiously googling tuberculosis on his BlackBerry. I speed read the tiny text and feel my shoulders relax. The results are remarkably calming. Tuberculosis is widespread and, with a two-year course of antibiotics, totally curable. An old memory surfaces and I remember that my own father had tuberculosis when he was a boy in times that were much less advanced medically and he is leading a long and healthy life. 'Everything is going to be ok,'

I soothe myself and Alastair, who is now moving in and out of consciousness. New diagnosis. Curable diagnosis. Another blessed stepping stone.

A male doctor enters the room at speed. He is short, with a matted blond ponytail. I am beginning to lose track of doctors now. There seems an endless stream of them coming briefly in and out. Nobody seems to be in charge. He does not address Alastair, but looks directly at me. 'We are going to have to intubate your husband,' he says. He turns his back to me and begins to prepare the tray for intubation with the help of a stocky nurse.

'Is this totally necessary?' I address his back, my voice terse with frustration. The doctor stops his preparation and turns to look at me directly. In a slow, definite drawl he says to me, 'Ma'am, your husband is gravely ill.'

I listen without hearing. Americans! I think in my inner monologue. They are so melodramatic.

As the doctor begins to intubate, I stand away from the bed to give him space. The clank of metal instruments against metal trays occupies my attention. The doctor bends over Alastair and I keep my attention on the tray by the bed. Suddenly, a squirting sound pulls my eyes to the doctor's back and I see specks of red spray across the room. 'Shiiit,' says the doctor as he continues to intubate through blood-splattered glasses. I am rooted to the floor, with my mouth agape. All stepping stones crumble in an instant and I am overwhelmed by the emotion that has been boiling up within me. I am gripped with a panic that bypasses my stomach and goes straight for my throat.

'What did you do?' I scream in a high-pitched voice.

The doctor ignores me and attends to Alastair. The question echoes through the room, unanswered. Finally, the doctor turns to me. 'There is blood in his lung,' he says curtly, 'and that's not a good sign.'

The sense of emergency in my body goes to code red. I am not sure if the doctors are with us or against us. I need to get help. I need backup. I run out of the room to ring Alastair's friend P and ask her to come to the hospital. I punch the letter P into my mobile phone and scroll down to her name. My fingers are clumsy and I have to do it twice. Damn, no ringing tone.

'There's better coverage outside the hospital,' offers the receptionist in a slow drawl. 'And when you're finished, can you come back so that we can get your husband's full insurance details?'

'Go to hell,' I swear under my breath, violently thumping open the hospital swinging doors.

As it turns out, it is I who go to hell.

The descent into hell

I live the manifestation of my worst fear over the next six hours. I had become aware of what my worst fear was a couple of months earlier. Since Tom was born, I had started to have feelings of panic whenever I was alone with the children in the house overnight. Alastair travelled a lot, and his travel always meant sleep-deprived nights for me. During the day, I would chide myself, telling myself that the panic was totally irrational, that I could control it with my mind and that this time I would not let anxiety overwhelm me. But as the evening turned to night,

I could feel the panic rising within me. I tried to drink myself into easy sleep with wine and watched funny, light films. I would ring my mother, keep her on the phone until she was nodding off to sleep and then put on the alarm and scurry upstairs. By two o'clock in the morning, however, I invariably had the two boys in my bed, with the door barricaded and my prized baseball bat under my pillow. Every creak and moan of the house was imagined to be the steps of intruders.

A few months before our trip to America, my mother-in-law had recommended a hypnotist to help me. I made an appointment and, when the clinic door was opened, I was surprised to see a tall, beautiful blonde woman in front of me. Her natural, down-to-earth manner relieved my doubts about hypnosis. The first thing she asked me to do was to describe my worst fear. I reflected for a few moments and replied, 'My worst fear is that someone comes into my house and that my children are suffering in the next room. I can hear them, but I am totally powerless to help them.' The simple articulation of this subconscious fear brought me a sense of relief. At the kernel of my worst fear was the idea of being powerless to help my suffering children.

A few months later, in this American hospital, I am experiencing the manifestation of this fear – but it is not my children who are suffering, it is my husband. His blood pressure has dropped so low that they cannot provide him with any pain relief in case his heart stops. For six hours, he writhes in pain as I try to help him find a comfortable position for his body. The nurse tells me to hold down his hands so that he does not pull out the tubes. I stand by his side, restraining him for hours, our eyes locked in mutual apprehension. P arrives and stands silently at the other side of his bed.

'Let the antibiotics get into your system,' I urge him, as I monitor his blood pressure to alert the nurses when it is high enough for him to receive pain relief. I am overcome by a pathetic powerlessness. In many ways, these six hours are like childbirth. Only twenty months earlier, we had been together in a London hospital. That time I was in the hospital bed and Alastair soothed my apprehension with his light-hearted banter. This time, however, nobody is joking and it is birth in reverse.

In the emergency room, we endure hours of joint battling and there is panic and frustration in my voice, in my actions. I pressure the doctors about pain relief. 'Please help him,' I beg. I cannot endure watching his pain and being so powerless to ease it. Like a first-time father during labour, part of me longs to faint to escape the experience. Alastair cannot speak because of the intubation, so I lean over him to try and understand his wordless gestures that tell me how to turn his body to make him more comfortable. He repeatedly points to his chest and then to me and I cannot understand him. I am locked into the mission of making him more comfortable. I cannot widen my perception beyond that.

Exasperated, Alastair suddenly stops writhing and his body slumps away from me. His eyes go through my head. His look drains of recognition of me and fills with wide-eyed shock. The machine starts to beep loudly and suddenly the room fills with doctors and nurses. I am pulled outside, saved from the stampede. A doctor stands in front of me in the corridor. I am inside my body and can hear the thumping beat of my heart. All other noise is muffled.

'That man is going to die,' the doctor blurts out, dragging my consciousness back out of my body. His words are a short, sharp slap across my face.

'Fuck off,' I spit at him.

There is an echoing in my ears that blunts out all background noise. I am in a deafening silence.

I turn to P and bury my head in her shoulder. The machine begins to beep loudly again. 'Be strong, be strong,' she whispers into my hair. On the brink of drowning, these words are an olive branch held out to me. I clutch on to them desperately and I am wrenched back into complete wakefulness.

'Can I be with him? Can he hear me?' I ask the doctor, who quickly leads me back inside. Alastair's heart has stopped for the second time and he is being resuscitated. 'Alastair, my love,' I begin, searching my mind for the right memory, 'Alastair, we are on our favourite island, Ilha Grande. It is a glorious day and we have just got off the boat and are walking over the hill to the beach. The sun is warm through the leaves of the green trees overhead as we walk. Now we can feel the soft, golden sand under our feet and we are coming out of the tunnel of green trees and can see the waves crashing on the shore.'

Alastair opens his eyes. A doctor by my side calls his name and he looks at the doctor, then rests his eyes on my face and closes them. His heart begins to beat and he stabilises. As the tension begins to melt from the moment, P holds my hand. 'I think he was saying, "I love you",' she said. 'When he was pointing at his chest and then at you, I think he was saying, "I love you".'

Gut-feel

Outside, morning turns to afternoon, with the usual callousness of time. Inside the hospital, where we have now been for over twelve hours, time plays tricks on us. The windowless emergency room, with its unnaturally bright lights, gives no hint of the time of day. Some moments seem like time-warped eternities, while others skip by in a flush of nonchalance. We enter into a game of cat and mouse with Alastair's vital signs and the weather. Alastair has to stabilise sufficiently to be transferred by helicopter to the University Hospital in Stanford, where he will receive the best care. In addition, the San Francisco mist has settled over the bay and is making helicopter travel dangerous. It has to lift sufficiently for Alastair to be transferred.

He is unconscious now, but I know he can hear me. I sit beside him, in an intimacy unabashed by the myriad of doctors and nurses around us. I tell him stories – stories of his childhood, his family and his friends, about how we met, about our wedding, the boys and our adventures together. This is the moment of the open heart, of all secrets revealed.

'Remember when we were both at a big conference in Oxford, shortly after we met and before we had spoken about our feelings?' I croon to him, leaning my face close to his. 'Remember I was sitting next to you? I felt this huge magnetic pull towards you and I found my body leaning towards yours. I nearly fell off my chair a couple of times. Remember you asked me quizzically if I was leaning on you and I brushed off the comment as ridiculous? Well, I *was* leaning on you, Alastair, I was. I felt this tug of energy and wanted to scream at you, "Can you feel this? Can you feel this too?"'

I live the memory of that feeling as I sit beside him and I search his unconscious face for some reaction.

'And when we were in a hotel on business in America when we started to work together and you were running late? You asked me to step into your room to wait while you finished getting changed so that we could go down to the team dinner? And everything was so correct and covered by a veneer of formality? All the time, Al, all that time in your room I had such a strong desire to jump onto your bed and bounce up and down.' I laugh as I admit this to him. 'I knew that we were meant to be together, Al. I knew it, even before the thought had formed in my mind.'

Story after story pours out of me and then I begin to sing him songs, our songs. I sing the chorus of Marisa Monte's 'Amor, I Love You', as the doctors and nurses work about me. I don't care who hears me sing Ronan Keating's 'Life is a Rollercoaster'. It is just Alastair and me in the whole world.

There is now a dedicated team of medical staff in the emergency room, where before there had often been nobody or just one solitary nurse. One doctor takes me aside and explains the situation to me. He strikes me as efficient and competent.

'Where were you before?' I ask, annoyed, 'before he arrested?'

'I just came on shift,' he explains half-defensively, 'but you dealt with other doctors.'

'I dealt with a handful of doctors, each with a completely different story and each passing briefly. Nobody seemed to be in charge.'

In the emergency room, the now-large medical team is going through what had happened that morning in the hospital step by step, detailing what drugs had been administered and when.

Anger begins to boil within me. 'I appreciate what you are doing for Alastair,' I say loudly in a sharp, terse voice, 'but it seems like you are more worried about not getting sued than saving his life. And, you know, who gives a fuck about being sued? Who gives a fuck?'

A hush falls over the room and nobody meets my gaze. Finally, one nurse puts her hand on my arm and says soothingly, 'Sorry if you feel we are more concerned about that, but we need to know exactly what doses of medication he has received so that we can know exactly what we need to give to help him.'

Bit by bit, Alastair's friends gather in the hallway outside the room and their chatter and occasional laughter are audible. They are on their phones, trying to find ways of getting the helicopter and the best doctors in place to help Alastair in Stanford. The sound of friends nearby calms me and a buoyant optimism and practical spirit is gaining strength within me. A female doctor tells me that I will have to change our airline tickets, as Alastair will be in hospital for at least two weeks. His kidneys have failed and he will need to be on dialysis. I sigh with visible relief. I can do this. I can change airline tickets. We are getting things back under control. We lost control there for a while and it was scary. We will talk of it for years to come with friends and family over late-night bottles of wine, as 'the time Alastair nearly died'. But for now it is over. As I talk to one nurse in fluent emergency-room speak, which I have picked up over the past fifteen hours, she smiles at me. 'Wow, you have learned a lot in one day.'

I look at her squarely, 'Yes,' I reply flatly, 'I have learned the importance of remembering how much I love the people in my life.'

We have moved from life-and-death emergency into recuperation. We have survived and now need to deal with the task of getting well. I ring my parents in Ireland, to ask them to come to San Francisco to take care of the children over the next fortnight while I am in hospital with Alastair. My mother's voice is bright and casual as she answers the phone, and she laughs as she mistakes me for my sister. I am aware that my phone call will crush this good mood. Before she hangs up, her voice has become tight with concern.

As afternoon begins to turn into evening outside, Alastair is stable enough to travel and the helicopter has made it through to the hospital. It takes half an hour to wire him up to the mobile machines.

'I want to go with him,' I state clearly.

'Can't do,' the helicopter nurse informs me. 'But I do need your signature on this release form.'

'Are you sure this is the best thing to do?' I ask, doubtfully.

'The benefits outweigh the risks,' the nurse says, seeming confident and competent.

I do not know what to do, but I sign the document. I hand it to her and say, 'I know he is unconscious, but please speak to him on the helicopter and tell him exactly what is happening. He likes to know what is going on.'

I bend over Alastair in the mobile bed and whisper to him, 'Please just stay alive until you get to Stanford Hospital. Then everything will be ok.' An image of our lives together comes to mind and I offer it as a final gift to him before he is taken onto the helicopter. 'Imagine the four of us on our balcony as the sun is going down on a warm evening, with the sky red and orange behind the park opposite our house. You and I are each having a bottle of beer and we are all eating Hula Hoops off our fingers. You are doing your silly coin magic trick for the boys, who are sitting on our laps and squealing with delight.'

Alastair is wheeled off to the helicopter for the thirty-minute flight to Stanford University Hospital, and Alastair's friends and I go to the car park to watch the helicopter take off. The relief is palpable. We are over the worst. I take Alastair's sandals and his fleece jacket. 'For when he wakes up,' I reassure myself.

As we leave the hospital, a male nurse runs up after me. 'Listen,' he says as he stands before me. 'I was here when your husband crashed this morning and I thought he wouldn't make it, but he has improved so much over the past eight hours. The colour came back into his face. I've been doing this work for fourteen years and my gut-feel is that he is going to make it.'

I hug him tightly and weep into his shoulder.

'That is all I want to know,' I cry to him. 'That is all I want to know.'

Positive visualisation

Alastair's friends and I gather around to watch the helicopter fly off into a sky streaked orange with the first signs of evening. As the helicopter takes off, I turn to his friends, buoyed by the nurse's comments and my growing optimism. 'Alastair always believed in the power of visualisation to get a free spot in a busy parking lot,' I remind them, 'so let's all imagine something fun we will be doing with him in a month's time.' I add with a smile at the small cluster of male and female friends, 'And I'm the only one allowed to think of sex.'

The laughter eases our tensions as we get into cars and start out on the three-hour drive to Stanford Hospital. I ring Alastair's sister in Mauritius from the car and reassure her that everything is going to be ok. The helicopter team rings us as we are halfway there to say that Alastair has survived the helicopter flight and is being brought to the hospital emergency room. Relief. With that, I try and rest in the back of the car, just forty-eight hours after Alastair was contentedly driving his sleeping family south on that very same road.

What's in a name?

On arrival, the size and busy efficiency of the hospital reassures me further. Alastair has survived the trip and is now safely in expert hands, with all the most up-to-date equipment. The hospital looks and sounds like a modern airport. The corridors are filled with waiting passengers, unsure literally if they are coming or going. Alastair's friend

K calls on the emergency room internal phone to say that we have arrived and they ask us to wait. I try to rest on an armchair, my body exhausted with tension, sleep deprivation and the lingering vestiges of jetlag. I close my eyes, but they will not stay shut.

I cannot rest. I want to know what is happening. I want to be with Alastair. Why don't they let me see him? My shallowly buried panic begins to rise again. I take the phone myself, saying that I want to see him right away. Reluctantly, they ask me to come alone to another part of the emergency department, where they say a doctor will speak with me. I walk alone through the hospital, disoriented and lethargic. I pass an old man slowly moving forward on crutches and I am palpably aware of his suffering, which I recognise as a mirror to my own. Then I see a young man with a face tight with dismay and I feel a physical tug at my heart as it stretches out to him.

In this great airport of a hospital, I wish I was walking towards a departure gate to fly far, far away from what is happening. I arrive at an open waiting room, with comfortable sofas and armchairs looking over the stairwell. There is just one small group of silent relatives there, who do not even look up when I arrive. I stand, waiting.

All of a sudden, I feel no hurry. I simply wait, all thoughts frozen, as time gently ticks by. Ten minutes pass before a grey-haired doctor in his fifties approaches. Hunched shoulders, I note to myself, as he moves towards me. He shakes my hand, introduces himself as Dr R and ushers me into a small room.

His demeanour is giving me all the wrong signals. What

an earnest face, I think as he asks me to sit down. I obey with schoolgirl deference, not allowing myself to translate his body language into thoughts.

'I'm afraid,' he begins with a respectful bow of the head, 'that your husband is dying.'

I hear his words but little do I know that it will take almost a year for them to seep in.

I react. I throw denial and negotiation at him. 'But,' I falter, 'he survived the helicopter flight. They rang to tell us.'

'Yes,' he says slowly, 'but he had lost his pulse by the time he arrived at the emergency room. We worked on him for fifteen minutes and he now has a faint pulse again, but his organs are shutting down and his heart is going to give up soon.'

'But,' I scramble again, shaking my head, 'he's only thirty-nine, he's healthy.' I almost spit at him as I speak. 'Two days ago, he was fine, absolutely fine.' I flail around, desperately searching my mind for a solution. 'If his heart needs help, then give him a heart transplant.'

Dr R waits before he responds. 'He's too weak now,' he says. 'Now it's just a matter of time.'

His words hang in the air, almost visible as they move in slow motion towards my mind. I fall silent. An eternity passes before I wind up the muscles of my mouth and whisper, almost inaudibly, 'Can I go to him?'

Dr R stands up and leads me silently from the room and down a long hall. I can see the open door of Alastair's room at the end of the corridor. As I move towards him, his body seems to be levitating over the bed, as nurses and doctors bend over him, resuscitating him yet again.

I stop at the door and look at his name written there. 'You've spelled our surname wrong,' I note bluntly and step over the threshold. Perhaps if I focus on irrelevant, small details, I can escape the reality of what is happening. Shock, it seems, is a closing off of my brain, a wall of defence against the unthinkable.

Alastair is bloated by antibiotics and he no longer looks his tall, thin self. As I enter the room, I hear a shrill cry from deep within me, 'Oh, Alastair.'

I feel an overwhelming urge to curl under his arm on the bed and fall asleep. 'Can I lie beside him?'

'Too many tubes, I'm afraid,' a nurse says as she pulls over a chair for me to sit by him.

His vital signs are stable again. I sit down and take his left hand in mine. His wedding ring is covered by masking tape and his finger bulges around it. I sit there with him, but there is nothing left in me: no stories to tell him, no songs to sing. His body seems vacant and alien now, soulless. I lie my head on his arm and close my eyes to what is happening.

Some of Alastair's friends arrive in the waiting room. Their spouses have stayed behind in the rented house to take care of the children. I walk back up the long, dreary corridor to meet them. We sit in a circle, shocked into silence. Our eyes are wide and ringed red.

'You know what,' I say to break the silence, 'I could really use a funny story about Alastair right now.'

They half-laugh, half-cry. J starts falteringly, 'Do you remember when Al drove all through the night to collect K's sleeping bag that she had forgotten for a camping trip and arrived the next morning, just in time for the twenty-mile hike?'

P interjects, 'Or the time he sold his car to some kind of gangster, who paid in wads of hundred dollar bills?'

M joins in, 'What about the time he spent a day at comedy driving school instead of paying a parking fine? He had to relearn the rules of the road from trainee stand-up comedians.'

We all chime in on cue, mimicking Alastair's voice, 'You can be right, and you can be dead right.'

We grow silent. A short, round woman appears. She introduces herself as the hospital chaplain and asks if we want to pray for Alastair. We stand in a circle holding hands, each of us saying our own prayer. I begin to silently rattle off a memorised prayer from my childhood, but I stop abruptly. Where is God? Where has God been today of all days?

'Would you like to come with me to administer the last rites to Alastair?' the chaplain asks gravely.

I look at her, feeling repulsion. She seems like the Grim Reaper himself. 'He is not dead yet,' I say shortly, 'he could still survive.'

'I understand,' she says insipidly, 'but the last rites are just to be on the safe side. Even if he survives, they will do him no harm.'

Her answer is a standard reply, offered, no doubt, to the countless relatives entrenched in denial. Reluctantly, I join the chaplain and we walk back down the long corridor. As we near Alastair's room again, my legs give way. A sudden, crystal clear thought has sunk its teeth into me: *Alastair is going to die.*

This thought has framed itself in my mind and a host of images flood and floor me – there are the boys, tear-stricken, there is his mother's face uncomprehending, there I am alone,

alone, alone. The images whirl like dervishes inside me. A cacophony of painful thoughts jostle for attention and I bat them out of my way as I stumble to the bathroom. I start to vomit and shake uncontrollably to the backtrack of inner voices heckling me: 'He's suffering,' 'There's nothing you can do,' 'It's all over.' Below this is an increasingly insistent bass drum-beat of denial thundering out: 'This can't be happening, this can't be happening.'

There is a nurse beside me. She's English and comes from near where Alastair's mother lives. Her forced chitchat disorientates me, but brings me back to lucidity.

Dr R examines me briefly. 'It is probably just the shock,' he says offhandedly, 'but these are the same symptoms your husband had forty-eight hours ago and we still don't know what is killing him.'

He signals to the nurse to get a wheelchair for me and suggests that I go to emergency admissions. I slump into the wheelchair and K takes me to the reception on the floor below. I feel an overwhelming exhaustion and a flat acceptance. Rationally, I know that Alastair is dying, but I have no urge to go to him. Where is my romanticism now? K wheels me along the corridors. 'If I am sick, bring the boys to the hospital as soon as possible,' I mumble. 'If I die too…' I clear my throat. 'If I die too, the boys go to my sister.' I curl up on a hospital bed, whimpering, 'I know what's to come and I just want you to sedate me through it.'

A nurse injects me and I tumble into relieving sleep. Time ticks by. These are Alastair's last hours on earth, and I am fast asleep.

Hours later, I drift back into consciousness to the sound of a Latino man being grilled by a nurse, who is trying to get his address or phone number. He is speaking Spanish and she is speaking English. I deduce that he is uninsured and probably illegal and he is evading her questions. I follow this soap opera for many minutes, before I gradually realise where I am. Some of Alastair's friends and a doctor are waiting for me to come around.

'Alastair is going to die soon,' the doctor says solemnly. 'Would you like to go to him?'

I do not have the energy to raise my arm, let alone get out of the bed. 'Can you go to him?' I plead to his friends. 'Please don't leave him alone.'

His friends nod solemnly in agreement, touch my shoulder and leave my bedside as I slip back into the escape of sleep.

In the early hours of a Sunday morning, Alastair's friends stand around his bed and joke, half-crying and half-laughing, with him as his heart stops beating. D suggests to Alastair that they smuggle him out of the hospital, strap him into a convertible, put a beer in his hand and drive him down the coast. I imagine a part of him, that part of him that is not in complete shock, chuckling internally as he dies.

A new dawn

I wake to a bright, new dawn. I feel rested and comfortable in a large, soft double bed, with glistening sun rays slipping gently through the slats in the white shutters. I can hear the squeals of children's laughter outside. As I gain a groggy consciousness, I recognise Tom's and Liam's voices among them. I stretch my body awake. I am midway through the stretch when the memory of the day before hits me like a leaden weight in the stomach. I curl into a ball to protect myself and gasp at the sharpness of the pain.

Alastair is dead. Alastair is dead. Alastair is dead.

The distance between the external peace of the morning and the internal turmoil is too great a chasm to cross. I need distraction. I pull myself out of bed and stumble out of the room into a large, pristine kitchen. Tom comes running in from outside. 'Mummy, Mummy,' he shouts as he runs at my body. I cannot lift him and slide to the floor to take him in my arms.

Alastair is dead. Alastair is dead. Alastair is dead.

Tom's innocence and playfulness dance from his eyes, as he hugs the mother he has not seen or talked to in thirty-six hours. 'Tom, my love,' I croak, 'you know your daddy was sick in hospital?' Tom nestles into my chest. 'Well, he died.' I blurt out the words before they can form painful thoughts in my mind.

Tom sits up in my arms and looks at me, for a moment appearing so much older than his three years. From some place deep within himself, he lets out a primal wail of profound despair. It rips through the pristine kitchen and bounces off the tiled floor. It is as if his body is making the sound that mine wants to make. I rock him, rock him as we cry on the kitchen floor.

In many countries around the world, a wave of shock and sadness ripples through Alastair's and my family, friends and colleagues, as they learn that Alastair has died.

No home from home

My family has always been a blessing: a typical Irish blessing. At its core are two united parents, seven eclectic brothers and sisters and their never-ending string of partners and children. I did not need Alastair to die for me to be aware of what a blessing my family is, but his death did put a spotlight on it.

On the very day Alastair died, both my parents and two of my sisters had rushed to America to be with me – one of my sisters had left her six-month-old baby. My parents were in the air before we knew that Alastair's illness was life-threatening. When they arrived at San Francisco airport, P had met them and told them that Alastair had died. My mother's legs had buckled from under her and she let out a shriek. My father had caught her as she faltered. By the time she arrived at a nearby hotel, where the boys and I had set up camp, she was speechless.

That night, D, a close musician friend from Ireland, who was on tour in the US at the time, flew to San Francisco to sit with me in silence in the hotel bar. I sat next to him, staring surreally into an empty fireplace, sipping wine and wondering where the fire has gone.

The next day, I go with my family to the house of one of Alastair's friends, where the whole group from the shared rental house have come together to spend the day. I sit on the edge of the pool, wrapped in Alastair's fleece, and watch the boys. They move from the arms and shoulders of Alastair's friends like a pass-the-parcel, each person lingering just a little too long in their embrace. They are thrown head-first into the pool and thrash through the water on floats. Their faces are alight with pleasure. Their holiday continues.

A friend of Alastair's sits next to me at the edge of the pool and hands me a cheese sandwich. 'I have a friend who has gone through the same thing,' she confides to me. 'She has two young children too and her husband just fell down dead of a heart attack one day.'

I wince at the thought of someone else caught in this deepening black hole and bite listlessly into the sandwich.

'She was really upset,' the woman continues, 'she didn't come out of her room for two weeks and couldn't eat a thing.'

Sigh. Reluctantly, I watch as this summons forth my ancient demons; the demon of self-doubt, the demon of inadequacy, the demon of comparison. Do I not love Alastair enough to recoil from life at his death? Where is my fatal romanticism, fed off endless teary movies and Shakespeare's romantic plays? Am I not reacting as I should?

I hug my knees up under my chin and pull Alastair's fleece around me.

I just want to go home. I just want to go home.

Surreal drama

Despair snakes languidly towards me. I hear the hiss of its forked tongue as I sleep. I wake, my heart beating quickly, and my instinct schools me in the first rule of suffering: keeping busy is an effective way of evading it. I click into automatic duty mode.

The first thing is to hold off the ominous torrent of despair. I go downstairs for breakfast with my family. I sit with my parents and sisters while the boys run around the dining hall, free and unfettered. I read a poem to them that I found by furiously googling on Alastair's BlackBerry.

Death is nothing at all.
I have only slipped away to the next room.
I am I and you are you.
Whatever we were to each other,
That, we still are.

Call me by my old familiar name.
Speak to me in the easy way
which you always used.
Put no difference into your tone.
Wear no forced air of solemnity or sorrow.
Laugh as we always laughed
at the little jokes we enjoyed together.
Play, smile, think of me. Pray for me.
Let my name be ever the household word
that it always was.
Let it be spoken without effect.
Without the trace of a shadow on it.
Life means all that it ever meant.
It is the same that it ever was.
There is absolute unbroken continuity.
Why should I be out of mind
because I am out of sight?

I am but waiting for you.
For an interval.
Somewhere. Very near.
Just around the corner.

All is well.

My family is silent as I finish reading. 'Death is nothing at all.' The torrent is precariously dammed.

Grieving on hold: tick.

'We need to take control of what's happening,' I say to my family as I put the BlackBerry aside. 'The Americans have been great, but they need to get back to work and their own lives.' They nod as one in agreement.

'We'll take care of the boys,' my mother says, looking over at Tom helping himself to a chocolate croissant from the buffet. Liam is sitting underneath the buffet table, eyeing an energy socket.

Childcare on hold: tick.

One of my sisters is in marketing, the other in financial accounting. The perfect death team, I think wryly. 'N, will you keep in touch with everyone at home, including Alastair's side of the family? U, will you help me with all the logistics?'

'Of course,' they both agree. How strange that I, the little sister, assume charge for once.

Plan of action in place: tick.

I ring my office in London and my boss answers my call with a friendly admonishment. 'What are you doing ringing work while on holiday?' he asks jovially. 'Aren't you camping somewhere in Yosemite right now?'

I bite my lip hard to keep from crying. 'I wish ... I wish I was camping in Yosemite,' I whisper to him in a low voice. For the tiniest moment, I imagine I am in Yosemite, with Alastair putting up the tent with Tom nearby. I exhale loudly. I mention Alastair's death rapidly, not wanting to make a big deal of it. 'I am calling just to let you know,' I say. 'I think we will need to put that deadline back a week or two, just while I pull myself together.' My boss goes quiet and signs off emphatically, 'Take all the time you need.'

Work on hold: tick.

Now I can focus on getting on with the new duties – the death duties. This first week after Alastair's death is filled with activity. We have to let everyone know he has died, arrange the logistics of getting his body back to the UK and make the first preparations for the funeral back home.

My whole self is shocked into intensely living each activity. I have never been as completely present in my adult life. The constant stream of my internal monologue has ground to a halt. I focus on each moment, each activity as if it is my last. I would never have thought that I would discuss at length the most environmentally friendly coffin for my husband, or liaise with my friends and family to find the right church, the right venue and the right band for his funeral, with all the fervour of an expectant bride. I hear the words come out of my mouth, but I hardly believe that I am saying them.

There is a continual flux of people coming and going in the hotel, helping out with all the tasks of the day: formally identifying the body, organising the viewing, planning transport and keeping the boys amused. We have endless meals and coffee breaks. I am complicit to the veneer of calm and the casual tone of the conversations, yet it shocks me continually.

We are at a friend's house in San Francisco, where we are holding an informal story-telling memorial service. Many of Alastair's friends have come from around the world. I joke that Alastair would be delighted that, even in death, he was helping to rack up frequent flyer miles. I joke, but there is hollowness to my laughter and to the laughter of those around me.

Caterers move quietly around the room, serving canapés and wine. A video-camera is set up in the corner, to preserve the stories about Alastair for the boys in later years. I feel faint and slip a canapé whole into my mouth. I watch myself making conversation. 'We are still in shock,' I say to myself, as I notice the wine glass shaking in my hand. A close friend of Alastair's from China appears, with his girlfriend draped on his arm. If he has come so far, it must mean that Alastair has truly died. My tears override my self-control. They fall in a hiccupping torrent and I am self-conscious of my own display of grief.

We are all in a surreal drama, playing roles in polite voices.

Unlikely answers

I need to know what happened. I need some bloody answers. We are still in the direct shadow of Alastair's death and do not know if his illness is contagious or not. Two days after Alastair's death, a panicked phone call summons all the children and adults who were sharing the rental house to a nearby private clinic to be given a shot of penicillin. Over the phone at the clinic, with Liam clambering on my knee, Dr R tells me that Alastair died from streptococcus.

'Isn't that just a sore throat?' I ask, sceptically. Dr R explains that it is a common bacterium which, in a tiny, tiny number of cases, can provoke a physical overreaction, whereby the body goes into sepsis and kills itself. 'There are approximately two cases a year of this reaction in the US,' he informs me.

I hang up the phone and sit back in the plastic chair, numb and silent. Liam struggles down off my knee and runs down the spotless, sanitised corridor of the clinic. It all seems ridiculous and farfetched. Two years earlier, we moved from Rio de Janeiro, half-joking that we wanted to live long lives and that a dangerous city reduced the chances. As I sit there, amidst the bustle of efficiency in the private clinic in a west coast city of prosperity and the American dream, I remember this and shake my head.

Both boys test positive for streptococcus. I breathe deeply and wait for the nurse to inject them with penicillin. I am too exhausted and numb to inhale any more drama. I call both boys to me and sit rocking them silently, blankly waiting.

The next day in Dr R's office, he shows us an article; a case study of a streptococcus death. 'In this case, although some of the care workers tested positive for streptococcus, nobody had any serious reaction,' he assures us. 'All those that tested positive to streptococcus now should be just fine with the help of penicillin.' The paper flops in his hand. I listen to his upbeat reassurance and wonder if Alastair's death will be reduced to a three-page case study.

T, a close friend of Alastair's who is a consultant doctor in England, has flown to the US and is with me to help grill Dr R and get some understanding of what happened. Not only do I want answers for Alastair, I am afraid for our two boys. Alastair's father died at forty-three, now Alastair has died at thirty-nine. Is there some underlying weakness in their immunity that led to these premature deaths? Is there a shadow over our sons' futures too?

They redo HIV tests, check for leukaemia or other diseases that could have reduced his immunity. Everything comes back negative. There appears to be no link between Alastair's death and his father's.

'Just bad luck,' Dr R surmises, as he shakes my hand in the hospital corridor to take his leave.

Conveyor belt coffin

Six days after Alastair's death, I am slumped on the floor of a small black booth in San Francisco airport with the two boys by me. Liam is crying hysterically, arching his back, and Tom is grasping my arm, his eyes saucer-wide with anxiety. Through the glass of the booth, I see my mother's face anxious and tight, arguing with the security staff, trying to get to us. A security guard bars her way with his body, with a look of practised nonchalance on his face. All sound is muffled to me and I feel a detached indifference to the scene. Even Liam's cries right beside me seem far off and cannot move me. Suddenly without warning, a clear gas is sprayed on us inside the booth. The whooshing sound of the spray frightens Tom, who lets out a yelp and grips his little fingers tighter around my arm. My body does not flinch.

We are taking a flight back from San Francisco to London, which has been arranged by Alastair's company. The last-minute purchase of seven first-class tickets has left the post-9/11 airport security staff nervous and they have isolated our group and are putting us through their most rigorous airport inspection. After the glass doors of the booth swing open and I pick myself and the boys slowly off the floor, I watch as a sober, pinched-faced security guard sorts through my hand luggage, each gloved movement slow and deliberate. She sifts through the baby bottles, nappies, two sets of house keys, two wallets and she fingers Alastair's glasses suspiciously. I observe her blankly. We are two-dimensional characters in a mind-numbing film – there is nothing human in our transaction. She pushes my bag towards me and I slowly fill it with the contents once again, momentarily tempted to hand Alastair's glasses to her as an act of surrender.

We settle into our seats on the plane. My parents fuss over the children, as they delight in the exaggerated gadgetry of first-class travel. I sit apart, disengaged. After the plane takes off, the alarm signals that we have reached altitude and, on cue, I stretch out my body-length chair-bed, swallow down two sleeping tablets on a dry throat, and curl into eleven hours of welcomed oblivion. Below me, Alastair's body lies cold and lifeless in the hold.

On arrival in London, the aeroplane staff lead us off the plane first and they whisper our story to ground staff. One member of ground staff looks at the children, gasps audibly and steps forward, leading us silently up the bridge and through to passport control. Heathrow airport is its usual heaving monster at dawn, with snaking queues of half-sleeping travellers swelling around us. The ground staff member curtly walks past a long queue to bring us straight to passport control. The children and my parents are in front of me and are whisked through. There are audible protests of injustice from the queue and as the controller looks at my passport, she asks me matter-of-factly, without making eye contact: 'I don't want to go into any details but, to assure the other people in the queue, can you confirm that one of your group has died and that is why you are being let through?'

I stare at her as the question sinks in. Images of the several emotionless security guards from this trip stop me sharply now and I am suddenly seething with anger. 'Yes.' I answer her loudly and tersely, silencing the impatient protests in the queues and grabbing back my passport. 'I can confirm that somebody died. As well as my suitcases, I will be picking up my husband's body in a bloody coffin on the conveyor belt.'

The bomb drops

From the airport, the boys and I go straight to Alastair's mother's house. I sit in a tight circle with her and Alastair's only sister in the peaceful bird-chirping beauty of a southern English garden and tell them each detail of his death. I am back in the confessional of my childhood. Forgive me, Mother, for I have sinned.

I feel an incredible guilt towards Alastair's mother for having allowed her son to die. In a way, it feels as if he had been mine just one week before, but in death, he became his mother's again. I have only seven years and his now non-existent future to grieve for, while she has thirty-nine years. I find myself mourning Alastair's whole life, including his past and future, not just the man lost at the time of death.

Alastair's mother was widowed at thirty-six with two small children. There is a bitter taste of déjà vu to Alastair's death and it brings to the surface much of her buried suffering from the untimely loss of her own husband. I learn more about her Tom in the days I stay with her after Alastair's death than I did in the past seven years of our knowing each other. Although we have always got on well, with all the usual delights and tensions of the mother-in-law–daughter-in-law relationship, we now have this monumental life-changing experience in common which gives birth to a new intimacy between us.

It is while I am staying with Alastair's mother that the bomb drops. Grief, exhaustion and jetlag have ganged together to wake me up to what has happened. When I rang a friend the day after Alastair's death, she kept repeating, 'This is the worst thing I have ever heard; this is the worst thing I have ever heard.' At the time, I thought to myself, Well, worse things happen; genocide, wars, devastating earthquakes. It is in Alastair's mother's house, after more than a week of busyness, that I realise that this is my own devastating earthquake. I repeat to my sister-in-law beside me, 'This is the worst thing that could have happened. The worst thing that could have happened.'

I slip into the cold clutches of depression. Aware of the children playing happily, it feels as though a bomb has exploded in our family and I am the only one of the four of us to notice. I crumble, unable and uninterested in taking care of the children. I am given more sleeping tablets in the vain hope that this will give me some release.

Most of the next day is a blurry haze. I am in bed when I hear the phone ring, muffled and far away. It is my mother ringing from Ireland, to where she has returned from San Francisco. I cannot speak with her but only let out a moan and listen to her cry with me. 'I want to take away your pain. I want to put it on my shoulders,' my beautiful mother cries. This makes me cry more. I cannot relieve my own pain, never mind hers. I listen to her voice until I fall back into my groggy sleep.

Death notice

After sleeping for a full day and night at Alastair's mother's house, I make the journey alone with the boys to London.

I just want to go home. I just want to go home.

The taxi drives us along the A3 motorway and turns into Wimbledon town. It makes its way slowly past the long row of Victorian terrace houses and stops at the one with the blue door, right opposite the park. 'I will be ok when I get home,' I say aloud to steady myself, as I notice my hand shaking when I unbuckle Liam's baby seat. I pay the driver and enter the house quickly, kicking the pile of letters and bills aside to drag in our suitcases. I key in the alarm code, close the door and breathe a sigh of relief.

The house is as we had left it just over a week earlier. My footsteps echo down the wood flooring as I move automatically into the kitchen to turn on the kettle. The kettle is unplugged. I stop suddenly. Was it Alastair or I who had unplugged the kettle before we left? I pick up the plug and hold it for a moment before plugging it in. I look around the kitchen at the papers scattered on the table, the notice board with Alastair's writing scribbled across it, Alastair's shoes in a corner with mine and the boys'.

The house knows nothing of Alastair's death. It is waiting for him to come home. It still thinks it is in good, safe hands. I start to cry. I am crying for the house, for its redundancy and the family it has lost. I so desperately wanted to come home, but without Alastair, I have no home. Alastair is home to me. Just then, Tom runs into the kitchen, with his bucket of Lego bricks in his hand and Liam toddling and squealing after him. 'Mummy,' Tom pleads with me, 'tell Liam these are my toys.'

I wipe my tears on my sleeve and retreat gratefully into the boys' world.

That evening, a group of friends call around and make a huge pot of spaghetti for all of us, shaking the house out of its mourning. The mood is flat, like the dregs of a birthday party where the party boy never turned up.

When most of our friends have gone, I sit down at the kitchen table with a close friend clamped at each side and try to write Alastair's death notice for the newspaper. How do you capture the essence of a man's life, a man you love, in a paragraph?

I begin with the factual and write down his age, his profession and list his closest family who mourn him. I include then the date, time and venue for his funeral and the reception afterwards. The text is void of life. A tiny, tiny footnote in history.

An image of Alastair comes to me and I see him laughing. How do I capture his laughter or the way I feel at his absence?

This is ridiculous. How can I be writing Alastair's death notice? I search my memories to add some humour to mark how ridiculous this whole situation is. 'Let's include that he was a two-time samba champion,' I say to my friends. They fall silent. 'Remember how he paraded with the winning samba school in Rio de Janeiro, two years in a row? And what was most bizarre was that each year was with a different school.' I am lost in the memory now. 'Everyone in Rio called him a *pé quente*, a lucky rabbit's foot, for the Rio samba schools. Hah, I can see him now in his mustard-coloured speedos and elaborate wings as one of the Horses of the Apocalypse. I can see him drinking a can of Antarctica beer and eating corn on the cob backstage at the Sambódromo, laughing and joking with his motley group of friends from America, surrounded by an explosion of colour and naked flesh.'

As a man with an Englishman's talent for dancing, mismatched with Brazilian enthusiasm, it had given Alastair great, great pleasure to proudly tell all and sundry that he was indeed a two-time samba champion. He failed to mention that he and 5,000 other dancers in the school shared the championship. He also failed to mention that these 5,000 dancers were glued together as they moved energetically for an hour through the Sambódromo in Rio de Janeiro, managing only to jump up and down in the cramped space and shout the words of the school's samba song at the top of their voices. All the while the sight and sound of them was being drowned out by the boom of the drums and the semi-naked beauties on pedestals. When boasting of his samba champion status, he would savour the impressed coos of friends and colleagues with a huge grin and would silence my contextualisation with a wink.

My friends exchange glances and one says softly, 'Write what makes most sense for you.'

I finish the death notice with a flurry of my pen:

RAMSAY. Alastair James, died tragically at the age of 39 on 27 May whilst on holiday in San Francisco. Adored and adoring Daddy to Tom and Liam, beloved husband to Bébhinn, son to P, brother to N and friend to countless. Alastair embraced life with endless passion and energy, living in England, San Francisco and Rio de Janeiro. Extremely successful partner, world adventurer, wayward athlete, incorrigible joker and two-time samba champion.

'You know,' says one of my friends reading the notice, 'had Alastair lived longer, I think he would have had a half-page or full-page tribute in a national paper.'

I start to cry gently as I put my pen and papers away. This chimes perfectly with my own thoughts. So much talent and ability, so much intelligence and energy wasted for no apparent reason.

The world is diminished by his absence. It has lost sparkle.

Last will and testament

Late that night, when everyone has gone home and the children are fast asleep, I am sitting bleary-eyed on the floor of our spare room, with open files, printed pages and cards scattered about me. After searching through various files, I find Alastair's will and tears drop on his signature, blurring the ink as I read it.

I have never read his will before and the first paragraph makes me cry. He requests to be buried next to me, if I go before him. Otherwise there are no directions for his funeral or burial arrangements. I have not filed away any conversations with him on the subject, from which to draw inspiration. I flail about in a sea of uncertainty.

The next paragraph of the will makes me smile. Unbeknown to me, Alastair has left 5 per cent of his assets to charity. I trace the letters with my finger, as I smile through the tears. It does not surprise me. It is completely in keeping with the man I know and love. Supporting international charity efforts is a passion and a life dream we both shared. Immediately, I am struck by the idea of setting up some sort of legacy or charity in Alastair's name, using his donation as a starting point.

As I stand up to make my way wearily to bed, I file away both the document and the idea before falling into restless sleep.

Awakening to the wake

The next morning, I am walking through the park in Wimbledon with my sister when suddenly my legs buckle from under me. We have been back in England three days and it is the day before the funeral. An image of Alastair's body has come to my mind and, for the first time since Stanford Hospital, I give serious thought to his corpse. Once he had died, it seemed an empty vessel. Even in the hospital, his body did not seem like him. I glimpsed his dead body at the viewing in America. Despite my request to the contrary, they put make-up on him and combed his hair to the side, hiding the naturalness of his death behind a veneer of preppy Americanism. Are we so afraid to face death even in its most obvious moments?

Beyond a muffled fear of seeing his coffined body on the conveyor belt on our arrival in London, I had not worried much about its transport or its storage in a local mortuary. Now I feel completely at a loss about what to do, with no cultural cues to help me deal with Alastair's sudden death. I am in England, not particularly involved in religion and there are many moments when a clear structure of mourning would be a great blessing. Although there is a strong Irish tradition of keening the dead, it is totally unknown to me. I am a complete novice to the ceremony of death. Suddenly, however, I have a thunderbolt of clarity.

'Alastair has got to go to his funeral from home,' I wheeze as I lean into my sister. 'We need to ring the mortuary and get them to bring him home. He needs to have his last night at home and go on to the funeral from there.'

My sister steadies me and does not question me. She calls the mortuary and arranges for his body to be brought home.

When the coffin arrives, the boys and I are out of the house. The idea of the logistics of getting the coffin in the door and Alastair's body slipping around inside the coffin makes me nauseous and I do not want to be around until he is safely positioned in our front room. After a while, I leave the boys and my sister in a café and decide to have some time on my own in the house before they return. I walk haltingly through the park back to our house. Watching the mothers with their children laughing and playing innocently, I am struck again by the surrealism of my life now. I am walking through this park, as I have done hundreds of times before, but this time I am going to see my husband's coffin in our front room.

I see the coffin through the front window. Its lid peeps over the sill of the window like a small, mischievous child. I run into the front room and grab at the heavy curtains in a frenzy. I tug them closed, nearly derailing them as I do. I want to hide this death. I want to contain this grief. In the semi-darkness, I lay my head on Alastair's coffin. A wail rises out of me. 'How can this be? How can this be?'

Gradually, the torrent of tears begins to melt the panic within me, eroding the tension wracking my body. Slowly, the coffin starts to lose its ominous air. I am struck with the sense of how natural it is that Alastair is at home. Having Alastair's body in the front room is not something to hide or of which to be ashamed. It is a vestige of Alastair. My spirit lightens and I carefully open the curtains. I put on our favourite Marisa Monte music with the chorus, 'Amor, I love you. Amor, I love you', and I sing it at the top of my lungs. I finally feel that Alastair is present again. I finally feel that I am present again to Alastair and that he is at home, where he should be.

All that day I sit on the couch, finishing our wedding album that I promised him I would finish, when we were on the plane to San Francisco. People come and go to say goodbye to Alastair. Death and crisis brings me into a simple closeness to those I love, and lifetimes of learned behaviour break down. My brother arrives from Ireland and hugs me with all of his energy.

'I just love you, Bébh,' he says as he holds me. I realise it is the first time he has ever said that to me in a non-joking way and I cry in his arms.

My father and I are side by side, leaning our elbows on the coffin in the front room. My father is a practical man, who is uncomfortable with suffering, eager that his children do not wallow in problems but think of solutions to get out of them. This time, however, he listens and talks in a way that lets the suffering be and I feel a boundless love and gratitude towards him.

Where are the signs?
As night falls on the day before the funeral, Fr D, a friend and enlightened priest from Ireland, who married Alastair and myself and baptised the boys, flies in from Ireland and comes to sit with me in our home in London. Fr D is in his mid-

seventies. His shoulders hunch over slightly, robbing him of the height of his youth. He walks in a gentle shuffle. He is present in every slow step, in every deliberate action. His eyes shine like those of a young boy. He has come full circle to his own innocence.

He sits beside me on the couch, with Alastair's coffin before us at eye level. We sit in silence. I feel his gentle spirit leave his body and settle within my own. Never have I felt such powerful, supportive presence without any touch or words.

Words tumble out of me. 'There has been a huge mistake,' I cry. 'Alastair should not have died. He simply should not have died.'

In life, I usually accept things that happen because I find subtle signs to tell me that things are as they should be. These subtle signs have guided me through my life choices and everyday difficult situations. This time, however, it feels like there has been a mistake, an enormous mistake. The universe is chaotic and out of kilter. Things are not as they should be, this loss should not be ours to face.

Just before we were married, I had given Alastair a leather-bound notebook to house his memories and dreams. In this book, all he had managed to write down was a list of his dreams in life. Some he had ticked off, such as 'having children', 'marrying Bébhinn, the woman of my dreams', 'galloping on a horse on a beach', but so many others still remain to be fulfilled. Alastair had so much more life to live and we had so much to live together. It feels like such an unnecessary waste of love, of talent, of life. This feeling weighs heavily on me; I have not only lost my husband but my sense of order in the world. Fr

D sits with me quietly and gently soothes me. 'The signs will come in time,' he says.

I allow his words to sink in. My mind goes to my meeting earlier in the day with the reverend who will lead Alastair's funeral mass with Fr D. Alastair's mother, sister and I went to meet the reverend for the first time and, when we arrived at her house, we noticed it was called Fairfields, which made us smile. This was the name of Alastair's childhood home, which his mother sold soon after his father died. As we talked with the reverend, the seeming coincidences went further. She had only taken up the post in this Wimbledon church two weeks earlier. Before that, she had spent ten years as the reverend of Christ Church at Oxford University. Christ Church is the college that Alastair had attended to read History and Economics twenty years earlier. As we talked to her about Alastair, about his life, his interests, his passions and his sense of humour, she went quiet.

'Was Alastair at a reunion at Oxford last September?' she asked suddenly.

I stopped to remember. 'Yes,' I replied, 'he was.'

'Well,' she said, 'I think I sat next to him at the dinner.'

I think about how Alastair met with so many friends at that Oxford reunion, how his friends from abroad came to stay at our house earlier in the year, about our skiing trip and Easter lunch with his family and even of how he managed to see his friends in the US before he died. Were all of these subtle goodbyes or mere coincidences?

I remember how, a few months before he died, Alastair had sat me down with the Excel spreadsheet of our finances. 'You might need to know this one day,' he said.

I had a quick look and dismissed it with a laugh. 'Alastair, there are things I do in this relationship that you don't need to know all about, and things you do that I don't need to know all about. It's a perfect division of labour!'

Five months before he died, I moved the television out of the comfortable front room so that we could talk in the evenings after he came home rather than fall asleep in automatic mode in front of the television. What prompted me to do that just then?

On one of these evenings, Alastair presented me with wine and several pieces of paper. 'Right,' he said 'let's think about what we want from life.' On each page of paper, he had written an area of our lives: children, work, leisure, family and friends, relationship, spirituality, and so on. He gave me lots of small, sticky strips of paper. 'Each of us writes important words about each of these areas and then we see where we have the same goals and where we differ.'

'Hah,' I laughed lovingly as I finished my first glass of wine and took the pen he offered me, 'the eternal consultant!'

There is a merciless battle raging in my head. The silhouettes of signs advance towards me, but I am loathe to acknowledge them. I am locked into another truth: *Alastair should not have died. He should not have died.*

Fr D's words ring hollowly in my mind, 'The signs will come in time.'

The last night

I am asleep on the couch in the front room, with Alastair's coffin next to me. I have put the boys to sleep upstairs and have come downstairs to spend my last night by Alastair's side. It feels natural and peaceful to sleep in the same room as his body. Half-asleep during the night, I hear the familiar pitter-patter of Liam's feet and feel his little body lift up the covers and cuddle in beside me. I am not sure how Liam knows I am here. He quickly falls back into deep sleep beside me.

I cry quietly as I hold him tightly to me; the three of us sleeping again in the same room, as we have done countless nights before.

The funeral: a flat, deflated smile

I am standing in front of my mother as she wraps a gold shawl around my shoulders. It is the morning of the funeral and I am dressed in the brown, crushed-velvet dress that Alastair gave me as an engagement present. 'You don't want bare shoulders in a church,' my mother clucks, matter-of-fact. I acquiesce. I know and care nothing for funeral etiquette. I only know that a strong wind could shatter me into pieces.

The boys' Slovakian nanny is walking them up to the church in the village, to tire them out for me. The rest of us wait for the hearse to arrive. Alastair's mother, sister and niece sit quietly with my parents in the kitchen. Alastair and I are alone in the front room and I sit down at the piano and play to him. My tears drop on the white keys, as my limited repertoire of Chopin and Mozart pours out of me. I am transported to the front room of my parents' house in Ireland on the day of our wedding four years earlier. There I sat in my sweeping white dress, playing these same pieces to ease my nerves before it was time to go to the church. The beginning of our marriage started in the same way it is ending, the similarities callously standing side by side, jeering me.

The doorbell rings and I am called out to speak with the funeral director, who has asked for me. He stands before me in a black morning suit, with a solemn, respectful face. He tells me that he has some important information to share with me. I move in closer to him. There on the step, while Alastair's dead body lies in the hearse behind him, he informs me that I can get a funeral grant from the government to meet some of the funeral expenses. The incongruity of the information with the situation of the day shakes me. I gasp sharply in disbelief, mumble insincere thanks to him and sit shell-shocked into the mourning car behind the hearse.

It is a glorious day in early June and the church is full to bursting. Perfect wedding weather, I note to myself, disgusted. The boys are playing with their cousins and Liam runs into my arms when he sees me. The music begins and Alastair's mother, sister, niece and I, with Liam in my arms, walk up the aisle. It is so reminiscent of our wedding march, with Alastair's family centre stage this time rather than mine.

I focus all my attention on the ceremony, not letting my thoughts bring me down alleys of despair or self-pity. This is a tribute to Alastair, to his adventurous life and the wonderful man that I was lucky enough to meet, love and marry. The ceremony is one of celebration and thanksgiving, with symbolic candles, moving tributes and soulful music. I read out a letter that I had sent to Alastair just before we were engaged.

Alastair, my love

*The times I feel a love that squeezes my heart and makes me
gasp for air are the times when you scrunch up your nose,
open your eyes and your mouth wide, and look in mock
disbelief, like a mischievous five year old. (This is often
brought on by Wolverhampton Wanderers or your chocolate
cheesecake, but occasionally by me too.)*

*The times I feel a quiet certainty with you are when you
challenge me and my thoughts, with such openness and love:
a challenge of compassion. These times leave me secure in
the knowledge that, with you, I will be the very best that I
can be.*

*The times I feel a great awe of you are when you are
talking and joking with people around you, especially
quieter or less confident people. Therein you show a respect
for each individual person you encounter – everyone with
their story, entitled to be listened to.*

*The times I feel a deep respect for you are not when you
show your knowledge, though I admire your mind and
your clarity of thought (most of the time) ... but rather
the times when you are open and truly listen to people and
forego 'seeming right' in the pursuit of wisdom and more
understanding. Your openness to new experiences, people,
opinions, ways of life refreshes me and excites me.*

*And the times when I most appreciate how lucky I am
that the universe conspired to bring us together are those
times when I can smell you and taste you and feel your arms
all around me.*

These are the moments that I realise that I have met in you my child, my friend, my father, my brother and my life's great love.

The children lay sunflowers on his coffin and gaily lilt, 'Bye-bye, Daddy', 'Bye-bye, Alastair' with all of their irreverence and innocence.

The ceremony is a testament to the beautiful man Alastair was. My teenage sister squeezes my hand and tells me, in full emotion, that it is the kind of funeral she would love to have. Later, my sister-in-law guffaws at this and says that the ideal funeral is a tiny one, where given your advanced age, only a small gaggle of your friends and acquaintances are still alive and able to turn up. There, the small group of stragglers would sit chatting and giggling in the back row of the church, sucking boiled sweets.

I wonder if it is better to blaze quickly in a flame of life or burn the wick to its very end. Or could there be a middle road of living out our lives to the natural end in balanced, homeopathic doses?

The children seem more capable of dealing with the situation than the distraught adults. As I watch the boys laughing in the church, I have the first inkling of how much they can teach me about dealing with death. We all file out of the church behind the coffin, as the gospel singers embrace us in one of Alastair's favourite songs, 'Swing Low, Sweet Chariot'. I imagine him in my mind's eye, doing the accompanying hand gestures and laughing cheekily.

Outside the church, people come to shake my hand and

offer their condolences in a surreal, shocked atmosphere. The sun is warm on my face and the churchyard chirps with the sounds of early summer. I see a cousin I have not seen in years. Old friends and family members hug me and choke back tears.

Alastair's friend P smiles at me through the crowd. She is wearing an orange shirt, breaking the sombre cloak of black that swathes all those around me. I smile at her pagan orange and unwrap the restricting shawl from my shoulders, my arms dangling bare at my sides.

We make our way to a room at Cannizaro House, where we have stuck up photos of Alastair at all ages. We eat canapés, sip champagne and talk about Alastair and life. Some of Alastair's friends start up a football match in Wolverhampton Wanderers' shirts. The shrieks from the football pitch are a welcome distraction and release for the emotion of the day. It is all so like our wedding reception, with almost the same group of people and that sense that I am moving from person to person, without the chance to speak properly to anyone. This time though there is no céilidh or samba dancing, no international singsong to finish off the night.

Colleagues of Alastair's, whose names I have heard over the years, introduce themselves in person at the reception. In hushed tones, they shake my hand and congratulate Alastair, through me, on achieving the difficult promotion that he had been anxiously awaiting.

The news, like the day as a whole, falls like a flat, deflated smile on my mouth.

Cremation

After the funeral, the immediate family goes to the crematorium to say goodbye to Alastair. I feel a flush of support in seeing all of my family around me as we file into the small chapel.

In his will, Alastair had written that he wanted to be buried next to me, if I went before him. But I did not know where I should bury his body. At thirty-one, I find it impossible to commit to where I want to be buried. I have the soul of a gypsy, always restless to move to the next place. Over the past ten years I have lived in Peru, Brazil and England, and I have no idea where the rest of my life will bring me. I suppose I would most likely be buried in Ireland, where most of my family and friends live. But Alastair has never lived in Ireland, and I don't live there now. It does not make sense to bury him there.

It made most sense to have the funeral in Wimbledon where we are living. This was where we had made our home over the past three years and it is close to where Alastair was born and raised. It was an easy, central place for most of his family, friends and colleagues to come. But would I bury him in Wimbledon? We had been ready to leave and had few lasting ties there. It does not seem right to bury him there either.

As I went through the options, I realised that it would be better to cremate him. By cremating Alastair's body, I will have more time to decide on his final resting place. By cremating his body, I can scatter his ashes in many different places, which is in keeping with his life and the geographic distance between his family and friends.

I have to override his wish to be buried. The situation is one that he had not imagined. I know quietly that I cannot blindly fulfil everything that we had planned when he was alive. The context has changed dramatically. I know that all I can do is size up each new situation and do the best I can.

This is the first decision I have made that is defined not by what he or we agreed before his death but that takes into account the new situation of his sudden death at thirty-nine. How many other decisions will be rethought and reversed in the light of his death? I think with more compassion about the decisions Alastair's mother made when she found herself widowed at thirty-six with two young children – decisions such as sending her son to boarding school and selling the prized family home. My life is quickly losing its black-and-white certainty.

The ritual at the crematorium also echoes with memories of our wedding, with the groom's family to one side of the chapel and the bride's family to the other. I cross the threshold and go to sit with Alastair's mother – the bride taking the place of the absent groom. The lilting, melancholic notes of 'Gabriel's Oboe' end the short ceremony as the red curtain is pulled around Alastair's coffin. This is the music that played as I walked up the aisle at our wedding. At this moment, one memory floods my mind.

It is of the two of us in St James's Park in London seven years earlier. We had just talked openly about our feelings for the first time. I had told him that all I could do in life was be honest and brave. 'My honesty is that I have never met anyone with whom I have such a connection in my life,' I had said, 'and my bravery is to admit that I am falling in love with you.'

He had sighed and looked out on the pond of ducks in front of us. 'Since I met you,' he said in a low voice, 'my heart has skipped a beat every time I've seen you.'

When we got up to leave the park, we separated, taking different paths. Alastair told me later that he had turned to watch me leave and said to himself, 'If she turns around to look at me before she leaves the park, then she is the girl I am meant to marry.'

Despite the sixty metres between us, I remember feeling his eyes on me and I smiled before I turned, sharing that knowing smile with him.

At the end, all I can think of is the beginning.

Part II
DEEP WATERS

'I have seen with my own eyes the
Sibyl of Cumae hanging in a jar, and when the
boys asked her "What do you want?"
She answered, "I want to die."'

From 'Satyricon' by Petronius,
as quoted in the preface to
TS Eliot's 'The Waste Land'

No solution to death

In the early hours of the morning after the funeral, I lie shocked into wakefulness with an empty space beside me in the bed and a vast sense of emptiness where our future used to be.

Alastair is dead. Alastair is dead. Alastair is dead.

If the first rule of suffering is that keeping busy is an effective way of evading it, the second rule is that when the busyness runs out, the suffering lands with a heart-shattering thud. Preparing for the funeral was a way of keeping close to Alastair. Here we were with a joint project once again. Finding the right poem, thinking of the right moment for the right song was an internal conversation between us. In some subconscious place too, I had been bargaining with Alastair: if I show you how much I love you by ensuring a funeral that celebrates you, honours your memory and involves your family closely, then, maybe then, you will come back to me.

On the morning after the funeral, I am racked with utter

despair that makes it difficult to breathe. I can only summon up the energy to walk around the park. I feel frail and breakable and need to be supported by my sister as I walk. I need fresh air but I do not want to interact with neighbours or any well-wishers.

When I return, my other sister is busy cleaning out my fridge. 'That's Alastair's job,' I note flatly. She hugs me tightly, and says, 'I'll come and do it for you once a month.' I smile limply, aware that she cannot and will not.

That night, I sit with a group of family and friends, all in our early thirties, on the balcony of our house, which overlooks the shadowy park. Aware of the vast emptiness that lies ahead of me, I ask each of them what they think my life now holds for me. They assure me that I can do my PhD, have an interesting academic career, fall in love again; maybe in three months, maybe in three years. They even suggest that I might have more children. Listening to them, I am struck by how I have lost interest in all of my earlier dreams. They are reassuring me that I can have a mirror of my old life back. I have the first angry glimpse of the fact that my old life died with Alastair: the ambitions, the dreams, the priorities. My former plans hang before me like drooping skeletons, mocking me from the sidelines. I can never go back to how it used to be.

I spit this out bitterly at my friends. One friend rubs my arm, saying over and over, 'That's ok, that's ok, that's ok.' I am filled with a sense of anger and sharp clarity.

'It's not ok,' I bark at her. 'You get to go home tomorrow and embrace your husband and say together, "How sad." But I will be here alone and it can never be ok. Alastair cannot come back. There is no solution to this. It can never be ok.'

I look through the dark out on the park, wrapped in desolate silence.

Ashes to ashes

Alastair's ashes are delivered late one evening, a week after the funeral. I have already put the boys to sleep, clutching desperately now to their daily routine of dinner, bath and bed to make it through the end of one more day. The boys seem so far away from me, even as I spoon-feed them and tuck them in to bed. Liam clings to me and cries despairingly until I allow him to sleep in my bed. He seems desperate to bridge the chasm that has fallen between us, to find me again under the veil of numbness that separates me from all things. I watch his futile efforts as if from a distance, unwilling and unable to meet him halfway.

I thank the courier gruffly, take the box wrapped in plastic from him and close the door behind him. I stand in the hall, remove the plastic and pass my fingers over the dark-brown of the wood and the smooth coldness of the gold-plated plaque that records Alastair's name and his dates of birth and death. There is a letter wrong in his first name and for a moment I think of running out on the street and calling the courier back. 'There's been a mistake,' I could tell him, 'this is not my husband, even the name is wrong.'

I stand there in the hall. Moments tick slowly by. The box is no heavier than a bag of flour. All that height, those long fingers, the green-grey of his eyes. This is all that is left now. I stand motionless, overwhelmed by hopeless despair. This sinking feeling in the pit of my stomach: this is hopeless despair. It swells within me, preparing to swallow me whole.

I focus on the weight of my body rooted to the ground through my feet. I breathe slowly, deeply to steady myself. And as I stand there, a sliver of relief comes to rescue me. At least Alastair's corpse cannot touch me now. The image of his body decaying in the coffin, the idea of the sickly hue of death on his skin had threatened to torture me in unguarded moments. I had fled fast and far from it into kinder thoughts, activities, wine bottles, sleeping pills. Now his decayed self cannot touch me.

Steadier now, I take the box upstairs to my bedroom and place it on the dresser, right next to the bed: the last thing I see before I sleep and the first thing I see when I wake up.

Single mother

I have entered a wasteland. My mind is constantly blurry and I am assailed by an interminable feeling of exhaustion that makes decisions and activities difficult. After several phone calls to my supportive boss, pushing deadlines further and further back, I decide not to go back to my short-term contract at work and the now-foreboding monitoring trips to the Congo and Haiti. I cannot shake the daydream of the first day back at work and the dread it awakens in me. I see myself walking through the open-plan office to get to my desk, amidst concerned and pitying looks. Even when I get to my desk I will have nowhere to hide. I arrange with the boys' nanny for her to stay on part-time for a couple of months.

In mid-June, my mother comes to London and we go for lunch together in Wimbledon village. It is just the two of us – no husbands, no children, no siblings. I cannot remember when we last, if ever, went out for a meal like this. I order two glasses of red wine and listen to her.

'We have all talked about it, Bébhinn,' she begins, 'and we think it makes sense for you to come back to Ireland. Bring the boys back to Dublin and we can help you raise them. You have so much family and so many friends there. The boys will be surrounded by all their cousins and uncles and aunts.'

I sip my wine and sigh. My parents have eight children, with a twenty-five year gap between their first and last child. They are in their mid-sixties and my younger sister has just turned eighteen. After more than forty years of bringing up children, they are finally free. And now I rock up with two fatherless boys and a broken heart.

'You can move in with us to begin with,' she continues, 'and then you can get your own place nearby. You were happy in Dublin before you met Alastair. And you are not alone now. You can come home.'

I start to cry. 'I have no home, Mum. Without Alastair, I have no home.'

I feel grateful towards my mother and towards my whole family. I also feel a sense of suffocation. I am no longer the twenty-two-year-old that left Dublin nine years ago. I have become so accustomed to living away from Ireland, to having it as my ever-available base. Ireland is my roots, but what of my wings? Do my dreams have to die with Alastair, our dreams to live in many different countries, to travel, to take on the world? Our dreams are not just Alastair's, they are mine too! If I was to go back to Ireland, would Alastair be relegated to a blip in my Irish life? I ventured out but I got bitten, so I recoiled into the safety of my native home. Returning to Ireland would be going back to a life before Alastair. Returning to Ireland would mean deserting the life we built and dreamed together.

'Thank you, Mum.' I smile at my mother through tears, taking her hand. 'I've been thinking about it too. I appreciate the offer to help, but I can't go back to live in Ireland. I am going to take the summer to straighten myself out and then start my PhD at Oxford University in September. I have to continue with our life, our family's life.'

I had thought that I would be ok when I got away from America and back home to London, but I see now how unrealistic that was and how little I understood about what was happening to my life. I cannot stay in the house in London, a young Miss Havisham eternally organising seven years of photographs. I need to move. I need to breathe. 'I will be ok by the time I get to Oxford,' I tell my mother, trying to convince myself.

During this long, lost summer it is impossible to grasp the enormity of what has happened. Each breath reminds me that Alastair is gone and that I will never look into his green-grey eyes again or hear his easy laugh over a new (probably pretty bad) joke. I need to will myself to keep breathing. I play back the day in the hospital and the months leading to his death time and time again in my head. The image of Alastair levitating in the hospital bed strikes me over and over at the most random moments, and I cannot shake it from my mind. I am on a ladder, where looking back gives me vertigo and looking forward fills me with despair. All I can do is focus on climbing one rung at a time. All I need is enough light to climb this one rung.

The boys give me that light. The daily routine keeps me busy:

getting up with them, dressing them, bustling them out of the house, dropping Tom to school, picking him up again, making meals, cleaning the house and reading stories for bed. The routine passing of the days enables me to put some space between the shock of Alastair's death and dealing with the consequences. On the surface, my life returns to how it was at the beginning of the year, before I had started working again. It is missing only its closing chapter of every day, where Alastair and I would sit together over dinner and share our days. I would offer up my endless activities with the boys as my contribution to the life we were building together. Now there is no one to share with, and our life is in ruins.

Below the surface, every tiny activity requires a Herculean effort. I am a swan on a seemingly calm sea, with a treacherous undercurrent threatening to swallow me whole. Even the simplest actions, like hoovering the house or making polite conversation, leave me feeling exhausted and I chide myself for my lack of energy. I fall into bed each night and fall quickly to sleep. Before Alastair's death I had found it hard to sleep on my own in the house without him, now I have no difficulty. There is no trace of my night-time panic attacks. Maybe after living my worst fear, it has lost its grip on me.

The boys seem oblivious to the colossal loss they have suffered. If anything, they are enjoying the attention that everyone is lavishing on them. They are kept amused by a constant stream of visitors and well-wishers and the endless conveyor belt of presents. Most of the time, they seem not to notice that I am in a haze, going mechanically through the motions of our lives. Time spent with the boys is bittersweet for me. They are one and three years old and they make new discoveries every day – new words, new questions. Liam sings his favourite song endlessly: 'Mummy, Daddy, Mummy, Daddy, I love you'. Their new discoveries delight me and I look around for Alastair to share them and I feel sharp pain at his absence.

The days pass with countless experiences that make me wince. I buy the new bicycle that Alastair and I had decided to get Tom for his fourth birthday and the salesman asks how good a mechanic his daddy is. I rush away in self-conscious tears from the fathers' race at Tom's first ever sports day. Tom and I are standing in line in the supermarket. A basket full of shopping hangs precariously from the handle of the buggy, where Liam is strapped in after a tantrum. I am feeling exhausted and want to get out of the Tesco glare and home as quickly as possible. I look at the queue snaking out before us and sigh. Tom tugs the jacket of a middle-aged man in front of us. He looks into the man's face and says with a smile, 'My daddy's dead and I'm not joking.' He has learned the reaction this story gets from others and he plays with it. The man gawks at him and then at me. He is visibly flustered. His look is a mixture of pity, scepticism and a distinct desire not to get involved. I smile weakly and try to keep it together long enough to pay at the counter and get the hell out of there.

The boys are a constant reminder of Alastair, which is at once a great solace and also a great burden; continually seeing Alastair in Tom makes me smile and wince simultaneously. Sometimes I need to look away, my stomach churning, when a casual hand movement or facial expression of Tom's brings Alastair to life before me. My relationship with the boys has moved from one of joy and lightness, sharing them with Alastair as the icing on the cake of our relationship, to one laced with a sense of desperation and neediness.

Just before Alastair died, we had begun trying again for a third child. My period is already late by the time he dies and days and weeks stumble past and still no period. A fantasy begins to take hold within me. Can it be that I am pregnant with his third child? Could it be that a part of him is inside me, growing rather than receding in presence? I did my first pregnancy test in the hospital on the night of his death, as the doctor would not give me sleeping pills without confirming that I was not pregnant. Over the following months, I take two more tests, each time hoping, pleading to see the positive sign of a red cross. All questions of practicality are absent from my mind. I simply long for one more piece of him. Finally, I sit alone on the toilet seat with my third and final pregnancy test. The long white stick mocks me for ten minutes with its one negative red line. I stand up finally and let the stick and the fantasy drop listlessly from my hand into the bin.

The inability to share with Alastair leaves me feeling alone as a parent and makes me doubt myself. A family member, trying to help, suggests that the boys live in Ireland while I get myself organised, and I could visit them at weekends. This fills me with horror: the idea that now I am less capable of minding the boys, that my emotional vulnerability leaves me unable to be their mother, and that people might think it was best to take the boys away from me. I fear that someone might whip away my life-saving float, just as I am drowning.

I recoil defensively and remember Alastair's words to me the day before he died – 'People must look at you and think, what a wonderful mother and what lucky kids. And they'd be right: you are and they are.'

These words steel me through moments of doubt and vulnerability as a new single parent.

Love without ego

Alastair is everywhere in the house. Where before he had been at work up to fourteen hours a day, now it seems as if he is constantly with me. His smell is on the shirts I bury my face in, his smile in the wedding photos on the mantelpiece and the curve of his body in the empty space beside me in bed. Alastair is a man I glimpse in the park wearing a similar T-shirt, a slightly balding head that I see in a car passing by the house. I ache to hear the sound of his key in the door and his half-sung, 'Hello, my love.' Sometimes I even hear the scratch of the key in the door and for the tiniest, tiniest of seconds I think he has come home. It sickens me that he can be outlived by his shirts, by his new, unworn jeans, by this stupid table we bought. I replay his phone message again and again, lilting my voice with his, 'Please leave your message after the tone. Thanks very much.'

He is everywhere, but he is also nowhere. I have very few dreams of him. By day, I go through the battery of monotonous tasks that is my life. At night, I pore over photo albums and replay home videos. All day, I long for bed, where I can conjure up Alastair's image and fall asleep with his memory fresh in my mind. But he rarely visits my dreams.

I am assailed by the feeling that we have had a terrible

argument, but I cannot remember why or think how to put it right. I experience an acute sense of abandonment and anger towards Alastair for leaving me. Of all people, Alastair should get in touch after death. We had a loving, strong, communicative relationship. He liked to say over a bottle of red wine that 'we have no problems if we can talk about them'.

'How can we talk if you won't come to me?' I wail, already on my second bottle of wine. Alastair was a persistent, determined man and he was very attached to his family. I had thought that he would move heaven and earth to give me clear signs that he was with me. As a teenager, I had sighed over the film *Ghost* repeatedly at sleepovers with my friends. In the film, Demi Moore plays a woman who is lovingly haunted by her dead boyfriend, played by Patrick Swayze. In one scene, he finds out how to move a penny and his ghost slides a penny up a door for Demi and hands it to her. This image haunts me. 'Where is my bloody sliding penny?' I rage.

I speak to Alastair endlessly, telling him that I am open to any kind of visitations or signs, suspending all doubt or disbelief in a clawing, clawing desperation to see him again. Yet in the darkest hour of the night, when the children are asleep and I lie awake, hearing the beat of my own heart echoing in the bedroom, my stomach lurches with dread at the thought of Alastair appearing before me.

I think about Alastair's friend L in America. She was not with us on our weekend trip when he died and had not known that Alastair was ill. However, during the night that Alastair died, L woke twice. The first time, she woke with the sensation that her husband was having trouble with his heart. The second time, she woke clutching her earlobe, where she often wore diamond earrings, sensing that she was losing something precious to her. She is a sensitive and open woman who had a lovely connection with Alastair and has worked through the death of close family members at great length. I trust her.

I send her an email to ask if Alastair had come to her in any dreams. This is her reply to me.

> *Thanks for your email. I will share with you a dream I had about Alastair: I was sitting under a tree and was feeling quite heavy with sadness thinking about you and the boys and the same perversity and injustice of life that you mentioned in your email. I felt Alastair hanging around and I started to cry. He said something like, 'I'm not sure what just happened. Where am I supposed to go?' He sounded so confused. And I said, 'You shouldn't stay, look for the light and go there.' But he said he couldn't, he didn't want to leave you and the boys. It was all a little strange and felt very incomplete. I woke up so sad. I, too, am having difficulty finding any meaning in this. One thing I know for certain: he is with you, unwilling to leave, and you will know that completely at some point.*

I read and reread this email. It chimes perfectly with what I expected from Alastair. I can imagine him stubbornly refusing to leave us.

This is just the wake-up call I need. I long for Alastair to be with me. I long for him to remain in some dimension between life and death, to shower me with love and help with the boys.

More than that, however, I long for him to be ok.

Wherever he is and whatever he is doing, I wish him peace and well-being. I wish him laughter and complete immersion into whatever experience he is having. This sensation is stronger than any feelings of self-pity. I imagine him meeting his father and his aunt, whom he had longed to see again, but not enjoying the reunions because he is so attached to life and to us.

I resolve to help him on his way. Each time I imagine him now, I tell him to go, to enjoy death to the full, to jump straight in as he did in life. I imagine him in a bright, yellow light of love and goodness and send him on his way. How good it feels to send him love in this way: a love so much more selfless, so much truer than the desperate need that was begging him to stay with me. It leaves me feeling lighter and dissipates my anger towards him.

I remember my words to him the day before he died, 'Al, I have the sense that our great life together will only get richer and deeper from now on', and I savour the uncertain taste of prophecy.

Love after death, I realise, is pure love. There is no battle of egos that is present in day-to-day life. It promises unbroken continuity and unveils the shallowness of death's victory.

Love after death is love without ego. It is a form of grace.

The providing father

Two weeks after the funeral, on a June afternoon, I am sitting at the kitchen table filing away a stack of bills. The day is warm and hazy, full of the promise of summer. I can see the boys through the conservatory windows as they play happily in the back garden. There are four opened bills with US stamps in the stack before me. I separate them out and wince. They are from the hospitals where Alastair was treated. The bills keep coming, threatening legal action in increasingly emphatic tones. When I had opened the first bill, weeks before, I had dropped it on the floor in disgust. The amount was written in both numbers and words to emphasise the debt: 'US$1,000,000 (one million US dollars).' No performance-related pay there, I think, with bitter distaste. I ring the insurance company one more time and beg them to make the payment and stop the bills from coming to my house. The bills serve up to me Alastair's death and our new vulnerability again and again, right on my doorstep.

It is like the funeral director telling me about the government grant on the morning of the funeral – equally incongruous and distasteful. Is money foremost in people's minds, even in these moments?

Just as I am about to dive into self-pity, a flash of clarity makes me grudgingly recognise that I am fortunate. The information about the funeral grant fell so heavily only because money was the farthest thing from my mind. Now, although the medical bills from the US are painful reminders of Alastair's death, they are not a noose on which my future and that of my children will be hanged.

For a moment I think of what it would be like if I had to pay these bills, if I had not been able to pay for Alastair's funeral. I shudder. I think of my brother-in-law's mother whose husband died in his early thirties while working on the docks and how she had to look after her four young children, pawn her jewellery and get a night job as well as her day job to keep the family going.

Alastair had worked for one firm for almost two decades, starting on a summer internship at the age of seventeen. He had worked long hours, but it was interesting and he was well paid. For years, he had been saying he was going to leave. It took his death for him to finally do so. With the money he earned, we lived very comfortably and had managed to pay off the mortgage on our home in London. As part of his package at work, he had health and life insurance.

Now the worry of money does not weigh on me, nor compel me to work long hours which would rob me of time to be with the boys or work through the consequences of Alastair's death. Even though he died relatively young, Alastair provided financially for me and for our two small children. I register this with a sense of relief as I tear up the medical bills and throw them in the bin. The logical sliver of my brain feels gratitude towards Alastair but the lonely part in me curses his blood money. I reproach him silently, 'If you had not worked so hard, if you had not earned so much and put yourself in such a high-stress position, would you be alive now?' I reproach him, but I swipe the credit card again and again with unthinking ease.

Later that day the doorbell rings as I am washing up. I dry my hands on a tea-towel and go to open the door. A leather-clad courier stands before me and hands me a package. As I close the door, I turn over the package and see that it is from Alastair's work. I rest it on the kitchen table and open it. Inside is a CD, entitled 'Alastair's Personal Documents'. I hold up the CD against the light streaming through the kitchen window and turn it in my hand.

From nowhere, the thought enters my mind that he might have written a letter to the boys. Alastair's father had died when Alastair was five and his sister was seven. He had mentioned on a couple of occasions that he would have loved to have a letter from his father to guide him through life and that he should write a letter to the boys, just in case. I, of course, dismissed what he said and told him not to be so morbid. I assured him that he was going to live a long life, with the boys and me right by him to drive him crazy.

I walk slowly upstairs towards our little office, mulling this over. I sit down at the desk, turn on the computer, slide in the CD and wait as it revs into action. The house is silent and not even the children make a sound. I click on the CD and a long list of documents appears on the screen. I scan the list quickly and my eyes rest on one file. It's entitled 'Dear Tom and Liam':

Dear Tom and Liam
In a moment of paranoia, I am writing you a short note
in the case of what I hope is unthinkable that our plane
crashes over Siberia or wherever.

I have actually on occasions thought of writing you a letter
just in case something happened as I always wished that my
father had done that before he died. Given that it is late –
and I have all my packing to do – I am not going to make
this long as I, of course, hope that this never gets read.

I guess I want to say just three things:
1. You two bring me more joy every day than I could ever

*have believed. You are such beautiful, wonderful boys. I
never thought that it would be possible to feel this way.
And, after you were born, Tom, I thought that I could never
have as much love for another child … now you are with us
Liam, I realise how wrong I was and how my love has just
expanded for you both.*

*2. As I think about my life, I realise that I made many
mistakes. But the one thing that I know for certain that I
did right was to marry your mother. She is truly the love
of my life. Beautiful, passionate, intelligent, kind, caring,
creative and she has 'an edge' which I love – and she laughs
at my jokes. What more could I want? I hope that one day
you two find that someone special in your life. You just have
to trust life to help you find them.*

*3. I am so very sorry that if you are reading this letter I
am not around. I can hardly think about the prospect as
I sit here. I am so looking forward to seeing you grow up.
My one wish for you is to enjoy life and be happy: there
are many different paths that you can take to achieve that
happiness. Have the courage to choose what you believe is
right for you, and trust your gut-feel – it never let me down
when I really listened to it.*

*There is so much more I want to say but I hope these are
words that you never read.*

I will always be with you in spirit.

I fall back into the chair and let out a cry. It is a letter from
beyond death. It is short and sweet, capturing the core of what
Alastair needs his sons and me to know.

This man, who welcomed our children with such love and organised for them financially and materially, followed his gut-feel to provide for them emotionally as well.

Identity crisis

As well as Alastair's death, I am experiencing my own personal little deaths day by day – the death of my place in society and the death of my own self-image. I am quickly losing all that I was – an independent woman, a beloved wife, a part of a strong couple raising our children, a supportive friend. I tick the 'widow' box in form after form and shudder. Goals that my ego held as important, such as developing my career, using my academic potential, carving out my own individuality from my children and husband, being someone and doing great things in the world, lose all meaning. I have no interest in world affairs and watch our weekly copies of *The Economist* pile up by the door, still in their plastic sleeves. I have fallen out of a race that I was having with myself. I am crouched naked amidst the ashes of who I used to be.

Losing Alastair leaves me at sea in a myriad of ways. Suddenly, all the things that he used to do, from mowing the lawn, to booking flights, to bringing the boys swimming, to doing the tax returns, fall to me. I remember his defensive voice during an argument before he died, as he said, 'Hey, I do a lot for this family.' I am ashamed and humbled by how much I had taken for granted. I am swamped in administrative to-dos. The last thing I want to do is change bills from his name into mine, deal with his medical bills or health insurance or initiate the process of probate (which I have never heard of before). 'But these are Alastair's jobs,' I whine to myself late at night in the office, trying to make sense of the different files and emails. I met Alastair in my first year of work and he had always done my tax returns for me. Now I am being asked to do multiple tax returns and I do not know where to begin. I have help from Alastair's old firm and have access to an accountant and a lawyer, but a huge amount of the paperwork still falls to me.

I set about these tasks with all the reluctance I can muster. I ring the utility companies to change the name on our bills, informing them of Alastair's death, and only one of them offers their condolences. The cold efficiency with which these companies meet the information I give them leaves me angry. Are we really in an emotionless world, where efficiency is more important and more natural than compassion?

In the midst of all these new and old demands, I feel incredibly supported after Alastair's death. My family and friends and everyone in any way connected with me, Alastair or my family rally around in an incredible way. I can palpably feel their well-wishing. My family travels to see me, listens with infinite patience, sends me books and poems and helps with the boys. Friends come for tea after busy days at work, call into the house with bars of chocolate to check I am ok and shower the boys in unnecessary presents. My close friend C keeps pace with me, as I devour book after book on loss and death. She listens to my thoughts, compassionately questions my often self-pitying thinking and shares her own questions and understanding. She shows me that the only thing you can do for a friend who is suffering is live the line: 'You are not alone – I am with you.'

As well as being supportive, however, people are giving advice and entering into my affairs in a way that they would never have done if Alastair had been there. It is as if all of the security and strength of our nuclear family has disintegrated. I feel that people no longer believe I am strong and competent. My sister-in-law, who had asked Alastair (and me by proxy) to be a guardian of her children in the event of her death, asks someone else to take on the role. I realise no one will ever ask me now to act as guardian to their children. I have no left-over love and security to offer. I am the one now to be helped, the poor one.

There is no right thing for anyone to say. I am in a sea of vulnerability and sensitivity and every remark, every action, triggers a defensive reaction in me. Friends and acquaintances tell me how, when they are having a bad day with the kids or at work, they think of me and thank God for all they have. They are learning to appreciate life at the expense of my family. Should I feel glad that my life, my broken, pitiful life, gives them the perspective to be more grateful for their own blessings? I hate when they talk of this, and yet I hate it more when they do not talk of this. I cannot abide the endless moaning about the day-to-day trivialities of family life. As I watch my friends continue in their uninterrupted everyday, toying with having another child, making plans for the summer or for next year, I secretly long to bark at them, 'Don't be so cocksure.' I long to growl, 'Do you think that you have escaped life's bitterness? I too was appreciative. I too was grateful for my lot and look what it brought me. Life is as ephemeral as a wisp of smoke; don't build your dreams on it.'

I bite my tongue again and again. So often, it feels like

talking about child-rearing with someone who has never reared a child. I calculate how long it will take until each friend is in my situation, with two children aged one and three. Just as they reach that stage, I will stand beside them and whisper in their ear out of the blue, 'Now, imagine how your life would be if your husband died today and never came home again. That is what I experienced.' Maybe then they will have some tiny taste of what I feel.

People tell me that I will have to now be both mother and father to the boys. This is overwhelming at a time when I am still finding it hard to make out the words in their night-time stories.

Early one morning in mid-June, I cannot sleep. I go outside and begin to mow our small lawn with our manual lawnmower. It has not been cut since Alastair's death and it is my first time ever cutting it. I puff as I go, cursing the blunt blades and leaving the lawn in a complete mess. As I sit in the kitchen, drinking a hot cup of coffee and looking out at the badly shorn lawn, one thing becomes clear to me: if I try to do everything that Alastair did, I will not be able to do what I did. If I try to be mother and father to the boys, then they will lose their mother as well as their father. It is enough of a challenge to be myself, as authentically and fully as possible.

As I finish my coffee, it is clear to me that I need to concentrate on the essentials and outsource wherever friendships and finances allow. Mustering up enough self-love and humility to truly accept my own day-to-day limitations and vulnerability and to accept the help offered so openly by those around me will no doubt take much longer than a cup of coffee however.

Desperately seeking solutions I

My mind is tight with a clawing desperation to deal with what has happened. I want to return to the way life was and to restore a sense of security.

I flail around, looking for some form of life raft to help me deal with the situation. At the end of June, I decide to follow through on a decision I had made almost ten years earlier, when I was on the St James's Way pilgrimage. As a single and footloose twenty-three-year-old, I had promised myself that if anything ever went wrong in my life, I would retreat to the pilgrimage.

Now as a widow with two small boys, the idea of leaving them is simply unbearable. Why not saddle up the double-seated pushchair and bring them along? I could do a shorter version of the pilgrimage with them. I google the pilgrimage and find one of the paths is called the English Way and is just over 100 kilometres long. Surely we could do that one in honour of Alastair? That way, we can also spread some of his ashes on arrival in the cathedral square in Santiago, the so-called field of stars, as he had always said he wanted to walk the pilgrimage of our cupid saint with me. My parents, who walked the pilgrimage a few years ago and know the type of terrain and the simplicity of the hostels on the way, gently question how feasible it will be with two young children.

'At least let us come with you to help carry the pushchair over any obstacles in the way,' my father pleads.

'No, Dad,' I assure him, uncertain of my motives, 'we need to do this alone.'

A month after Alastair's death, I go online and book our

flights. This plan gives me a sense of peace, another distraction for my mind and another way of keeping Alastair close. After an interminable month of feeling completely out of control of my life, I am taking the reins again. Perhaps that is why I do not ask my parents to join us. Perhaps I need to feel fully in control of some small thing, rather than slipping into adaptive daughter mode.

For the next couple of days I keep my eyes open for a scallop shell, the symbol of the pilgrimage. The last time I did the pilgrimage, I had found my shell in Peru and it had been the sign I needed to embark on the walk. This time I look for confirmation that going on pilgrimage is the right thing to do. Finding the shell would be the perfect sign.

I do not find a shell before I go.

The night before our trip, I wait until the boys are asleep and then take the wooden box of Alastair's ashes off my side-table by the bed and walk downstairs. I hold the box out before me with ceremonial reverence. I put the CD of our wedding song 'Gabriel's Oboe' in the CD player. As the music echoes through me, I slowly unscrew each of the six screws that hold on the top of the box. Then, through tears, I spoon some of his ashes into a little wooden box, hand-painted with flowers. We got the box, which originally contained mints, at our friends' wedding the week before Alastair died. 'These could come in useful,' Alastair had smiled as he popped them into his pocket at the end of the night. Little did he know that, a month later, this small box would hold his ashes.

The next morning, the boys and I are relaxed on the plane journey and I am calmly taking one step at a time. We find our hotel in Santander and drop off our bags. Then the three of us go looking for something to eat, pretending to be the three billy goats gruff. I am filled with a sense of strength as we walk and play: I can travel on my own with the boys, I can continue to have adventures, I can still feel alive.

It is just at that moment that Liam, in his one-year-old curiosity, levers himself up onto a low ledge, loses his footing and bangs his face. His howl pierces the calm. I wipe the blood from his face and kiss away his tears. Slowly and silently, he opens my hand and places one perfect baby front tooth into it.

I stare at the tooth in horror. It represents his innocence – the former perfection of his young life – and brings me back to earth with a sharp thud. I pull the boys into a nearby café and ask for a glass of milk to put the tooth in. In a panicked voice, I ask them to call a taxi to bring us to the nearest hospital. When we arrive, I use my rusty Spanish to explain the situation and the receptionist points us to the waiting room.

In a red plastic chair in the hospital waiting room, I weep quietly and desolately, as the boys play at my feet. Here I am again, one month later, in a foreign country, in a hospital waiting room. A refrain, reminding me of a line from a Simon and Garfunkel song, plays, on constant repeat, in my mind: *'Why have you forsaken me?'*

After waiting for four hours I am called forward and explain the situation, in broken Spanish, to the attending nurse. She looks at me as if I am crazy and tells me that the tooth cannot be put back in and that it will grow again in five or six years. I inarticulately tell her of Alastair's death and how I need to be sure that Liam's mouth will not get infected. I am looking for compassion, but she sidesteps my drama like a seasoned pro. 'Nada que hacer,' she says deliberately to me and points to the door. Yes – nothing to be done indeed.

I bundle a tired Liam in my arms and take Tom's chubby little hand in mine. We leave the hospital and return to our three-star hotel. In the hotel room, I push the two single beds together so that we can all sleep huddled up. As the boys fall sleep at each side of me, I stay awake to read the full story of Job for the first time. I identify with this man who was sent layer after layer of suffering and I falter between self-pity and determination.

Becoming pilgrims

The broken tooth does not deter me. I am not listening to this clear sign. We take a train to the beginning of the English Way in the northwest corner of Spain. I push an unco-operative double buggy laden with bags along uneven woodland passes, steep hills and motorway hard shoulders. All the while, I bribe the boys with lollipops and ice-creams to stay sitting. By the time we arrive at the hostels, the boys are buzzing with sugar and a day trapped in the buggy and are eager to expend all of their energy running around. I am, of course, physically exhausted.

During the first two nights, we stay in the official pilgrim hostels. We arrive at the first of these hollow shells of buildings – brick placed lacklustre on top of brick as a soulless, municipal duty. It is in the middle of a long, sparse public park. There are no other buildings for 500 metres. We pull at the doors that are locked tightly shut. I prop the boys up to un-curtained windows to peer in, but there is no movement, no life inside. I find an uninviting message pasted next to the door, informing me of a mobile phone that I can call to speak to some distant reception. I ring the number and speak with a formal municipal official. After waiting half an hour, he arrives to open the door for us. He shows little interest in the pilgrimage or these three unlikely pilgrims. He languidly opens the door, shows me how to turn on the lights and emphasises that I am to pull the door shut on our departure.

'Will there be nobody else sleeping here with us?' I ask, apprehensively.

He looks at me and sighs in slow Spanish, 'This part of the St James's Way is not very popular. And you are out of the high season of July and August,' he adds accusingly. 'If you need help, you can call this phone number until six o'clock. Otherwise call the police.' He leaves without looking back.

I lie restless in a single bunk, with Liam by my side. It is difficult to sleep alone with the two boys in this desolate building, far from the reassuring sounds of the town. 'Please keep us safe, Alastair,' I whisper into the darkness, like an endless mantra. This pilgrimage is nothing like the full French Way that I had followed a decade ago. No diving into presence, no spiritual rituals, no support from other pilgrims. Indeed, no other pilgrims. As I lie there in the darkness, listening to the sound of Tom's rhythmic breathing in the bunk above me, one question comes to me, 'What the hell am I doing here?'

On day three, after an eight-kilometre walk punctuated by ice-cream bribes and uneven forest paths, we arrive at a town with no pilgrims' hostel. We find instead a small hotel. As soon as we enter, the boys spy a pool and demand to go for a swim. I check in and we quickly climb the stairs to leave our bags in our room. With our swimming costumes over my shoulder, we rush back downstairs to the pool. The pool is about ten metres long and two metres deep. I notice with dismay that it is too deep for me to stand, making it impossible to hold on to both small boys at the same time. Neither of them can swim independently and I have no armbands or floats. For a fraught five minutes, I try to take one at a time into the water, while the other waits on the steps until I return. As I swim out with Liam, Tom grows impatient and jumps into the water after me. I grab him to stop him from going under. I nearly sink under the weight of the two of them and both swallow water. I kick my legs furiously to get to the steps and drop the two shocked boys, before gasping for air myself. 'That's it,' I rant breathlessly. 'I've had enough. I can't do this on my own.'

I leave the pool, dragging the two unwilling, crying boys behind me. I am completely alone. 'Where are you, Alastair?' I wail within myself, as so many times before. 'You should not have died. You should not have died. I need you here.'

In the ensuing silence, I face with despair the inexorable limitations of being a single mother with two small boys.

I wrap the boys in towels and we make our way noisily back to our room. As we pass through the foyer, something colourful on a side table catches my eye. I stop and look closer. It is a scallop shell, the pilgrims' symbol, and each groove is painted a different, bright colour by a child's hand. The shell is perfect for our kid pilgrimage. I pick it up and hold it out to the boys.

'Our shell!' I laugh to the boys. 'We've found our pilgrim shell.' The boys look closely at the rainbow-coloured shell and smile at me with tear-stained faces. Tom picks up the shell and turns it around in his open, little hand.

'*Now* we are pilgrims,' I laugh at the boys, as we shiver together in the foyer.

The sky falls down

The following day, I strap the rainbow shell on the double buggy and push the boys across a bridge, past an eerie old tower and up over the hills to the next town. The day is glorious and we stop for lunch near a beach and play for a few hours in the hot sun, writing love messages with sticks and stones for Alastair in the sand. Then I saddle the boys into the buggy again and push them for four hours uphill. The trail is too difficult for the buggy, so I find myself pushing them on the hard shoulder of a busy road as cars zoom past centimetres away. A mixture of exhaustion and fear for our lives sobers me. The baby-pushing part of this pilgrimage is reaching its end. I interpret the finding of the shell as a sign that we have come far enough and have earned our pilgrim stripes.

This is confirmed by the next town into which our unlikely troupe trundles.

We arrive at early evening. The pilgrims' hostel is being renovated and we have to find somewhere else to stay. I push the buggy up the seventy-degree hill to the main street and start to look for a room for the night. However, we have arrived on the town's annual holiday, and there is literally no room at the inn. I go to each one of the five pubs and guest houses along the main road and am met with offhand dismissal at each one. The boys are restlessly bouncing in the buggy, which is packed on each side by paddle bags full of clothes, plastic bags of food knotted to the handle and draped all over with the children's wet clothes, which I had washed that morning and am trying to dry as we walk. Tom starts to bang an empty tin that a shopkeeper had given him to keep him occupied. We are a bedraggled noise, drawing looks from every side as we career along the pavement.

Suddenly, a car pulls sharply in front of us and makes me pull the handbrake on the buggy to avoid an accident. I gasp audibly and stare in angry disbelief at the young couple in the front of the car, who have pulled up onto the curb to turn around. I watch as the girl in the passenger seat points us out to the driver, indicating for him to take care. The young man looks up at me and his eyes go to the buggy and the children before our eyes lock through the windscreen. '¿Ella?' I see his mouth say. 'Ella puede esperar.' She can wait. He gives me a look of contempt, smirks slightly and then slowly, oh so slowly, backs his car off the curb, finishes his turn and drives off.

I explode. A raging fire of anger flares up within me. I grab Tom's empty tin out of his hands and throw it down the road after the car. 'Wanker,' I scream at him as Tom's indignant screams fill the air. This inconsiderate jerk has flipped the switch of my anger and driven away.

I am once again aflame with that damning mix of anger and impotence – no one at whom to throw my rage. I huff heavily as the fire within me spreads outwards. I am angry now at the innkeepers who cannot find us a room and angry at the town for not having a hostel. I am angry at everyone who does not understand what I am going through. I am angry at the friends who never get in touch. I am angry at all the older people, the other widows and widowers, who cannot tell me how to get over this. And there it is again, that knot that will not unravel – I am angry at Alastair and I am angry at God, the two constants I always trusted to keep my sky from falling down.

Alastair should not have died. He should not have died.

'The only one who won't let me down is my bloody MasterCard,' I think bitterly. I hail a taxi to the next town and use the card to pay for a room in the best hotel, where the boys and I faint into immediate sleep.

The field of stars

I awake the following morning crystal clear that we have walked enough. Rather than presence or mindfulness, walking with the boys has brought me to exhaustion and despair.

We take another taxi to go the last sixty kilometres to Santiago. The distance whooshes past us, as we sit in the back of the taxi reading Mr Men books. We arrive in Santiago in time for midday mass. Midday mass is the pilgrims' mass, when the arriving pilgrims are welcomed and the enormous thurible is swung down the aisle on strong thick ropes. It spreads the spicy smell of burning incense throughout the church as it flies.

As I open the taxi door in Santiago, the first sound I hear is a Galician bagpiper playing on the cobblestone square. This reminds me of Alastair: his Scottish roots and the bagpiper piping us into dinner at our wedding. My legs buckle under me and I dissolve into tears.

I leave the buggy with a nonplussed shop assistant in a

nearby jeweller's store and enter the heaving cathedral with the boys. We make our way slowly through the throng of pilgrims and tourists. I have so little physical strength as I move forward, with Liam hanging off me and Tom wrapped around my leg. There are no seats left by the time we make it inside and I simply do not have the strength to stand. I sit on the floor of the cathedral, with the two boys playing around me, oblivious to the mass. I have no energy to keep them quiet. Liam's nappy has begun to stink. My body is wracked with sobs. I notice the other pilgrims looking at me and sense that they are chiding me for making so much noise. They have walked a long way to listen to the mass and here we are disturbing it. But I have given up even pretending to be considerate as I lose myself in my own despair.

As the service ends, we make our way out to the central square. I am quiet now, washed out by grief. Legend tells it that a priest dreamed that the body of Jesus's disciple James was buried in the middle of a field of stars, and the square and cathedral were built on top of this field. I stand in the centre of that field, paved over now with cobblestones and filled with a multitude of pilgrims, cyclists and tourists. There are no stars in the sky, only menacing grey clouds overhead.

As the boys lick ice-cream cones and run around the square chasing pigeons, I go to the epicentre. There I take the small box of Alastair's ashes from my pocket. 'At last we made it to Santiago together,' I whisper through sobbing tears.

I tap the ashes out of the box, sending him love with each weary tap. The ashes fall onto the cobblestones and are quickly lifted away by the wind.

Next of kin

When we arrive back to London, death is still lurking in every corner and I rush around trying to organise my affairs. The lawyers send me through the final version of my will and I print it out, forgetting it on the printer tray for days. Life is dulled with a hazy absent-mindedness.

Liam's second birthday arrives. The boys are out at a friend's house for the morning. In the kitchen, I put a tin of condensed milk to boil to make toffee for Liam's party later that day. I should leave the condensed milk for an hour, checking from time to time that there is enough water. Something else takes my attention and three hours pass. I walk into the kitchen and hear a sizzling noise coming from the saucepan. Remembering the condensed milk, I rush to the oven top and turn off the heat under the pan. The sizzle turns into an explosion – boom! The lid of the pan and flecks of boiling hot toffee fly across the room, staining the ceiling and the windows. I put my hand in front of my face to protect myself from the toffee. I register pain and shock simultaneously as my arm, neck and face burn. Screaming, I run to the bathroom, where I splash water over the burns. I fall down on the toilet seat and cry inconsolably. I cry lumps of burning self-pity.

As my mind calms down, I go out to the hall to get the phone and dial NHS Direct. I explain what has happened and ask what to do with such burns. 'I advise you to get to the hospital as soon as possible,' the male attendant suggests to me in a measured voice. 'If your neck is burned, it could swell up and you might have trouble breathing.'

My self-pity gives way to determined action. I call a taxi

and run upstairs to grab a pen and my will off the printer tray. The taxi arrives and I jump into the back. 'I need to get to the hospital,' I inform the taxi driver, 'but first, can you witness my signature on my will?'

I sign the document and then fold it through the division glass. He looks at the document and looks wearily at me. The speckles of burns look like large freckles on my face and neck and my wrist is wrapped in cling-film. He simply sighs, signs the document and takes me quickly to the hospital.

At the hospital, I am swept straight in to see the doctor. The doctor is a middle-aged woman, who moves with clinical efficiency. Her coldness makes me cry quietly. 'No need to cry,' she admonishes me as she checks my neck. 'You won't have any breathing problems and these burns will disappear in no time with a vitamin E cream.'

She performs an eye test, pointing rapidly to letters that I read out through tears. She picks up a form from the desk. 'I just need to get your full name,' she begins, 'and the name of your next of kin.'

My gentle cry turns into a deep-rooted sob. 'Who is my next of kin now? Who will take care of me if I am sick and have to stay in hospital? Who will sing to me when I am losing consciousness?'

Alastair should not have died. He should not have died.

I wail desolately, as a perplexed, impatient doctor looks on.

Desperately seeking solutions II

I sign up for a week-long silent Buddhist retreat two months after Alastair's death. I am not a Buddhist, but this does not make me waver. When I phone the organisers, they assure me that the silence will be holding and supportive. I leave the children with my family in Ireland and make my way to a big country manor in Devon, desperate for Buddhism to help me deal with the enormity of Alastair's death.

I drive through a twist of country lanes until I find the long, stone wall of the manor, which seems to bend over the narrow road. I hug the wall tightly and pull in to the car park. Even as I step out of the car, the silence overwhelms me. I am welcomed gently and assigned to a bedroom. I go to my room and I smile at the young woman with whom I am sharing. She nods back to me silently and makes up her bed. I move downstairs, where I noiselessly sign up for working meditation in the garden. As the rest of the participants arrive in dribs and drabs, I sit in the large, draughty drawing room, silently sipping mint tea.

The daily routine is exacting. From six in the morning we have hours of sitting meditation, walking meditation and working meditation. We begin each day in a silent group of thirty, sitting in the lotus position and listening to a short talk to help with our meditation practice. The talk is given by a gentle, Western, robe-clad monk in his early fifties.

'When you meditate,' the monk begins deliberately, 'you focus on the breath. You bring your attention to your inhalation through the nose and the expansion of your lungs. Then you bring your attention to your exhalation, as your lungs contract and the air flows through your nose.'

I breathe deeply and deliberately, almost in a sigh.

'Don't try to control your breathing,' the monk continues. 'Simply observe your breathing.'

I try to relax out of the rhythm I have imposed on my breathing.

For two whole minutes, I manage to observe my breathing and am flushed with a sense of peace. I am just here, breathing. Then the onslaught begins. Thoughts assail me. The external silence is a mask for the bustle in my mind, as thoughts compete for attention. Angry thoughts of injustice rev up: *Alastair should not have died. He should not have left me. God broke our family. Alastair broke our family by working too hard.* Guilty self-questioning rises up from below: *Did I break our family? Did I fail to save Alastair? Did I cause his death?* Pessimistic thoughts for the future drone on: *The boys will be emotionally scarred for life. I will be alone forever. I won't make it. I am not able for this.*

I try to suppress the thoughts and return to my breath. I manage for a few seconds and then the thoughts barge their way maliciously into my mind again.

'Don't fight against the thoughts,' the monk continues gently. 'When a thought arises in your mind, label it, imagine it is a helium balloon and watch it slowly drift away in the sky.'

Here comes my bleating chorus again: *Alastair should not have died. He should not have died.* 'Painful thought', I label and imagine the balloon drifting away. Before it is out of sight, another thought appears. 'Painful thought', I label again and now before the balloon is formed in my mind, another thought appears. 'Painful thought', 'painful thought', 'painful thought'. There is an onslaught of thoughts, they are ganging up on me, giving me no space to come back to my breathing.

'Sitting in meditation is like learning to play the scales on the piano,' the monk declares, dragging my attention away from my inner death by helium balloon. 'The objective is to bring mindfulness to every moment of your everyday life. With the practice of sitting meditation, it becomes easier for you to be mindful in the hustle and bustle.'

I never liked practising scales as a child. I always preferred to go straight to playing the music pieces themselves and improve as I went along. Perhaps that is why I never got beyond mediocre.

'Some people think of meditation as a hobby,' the monk continues, in a tone of disbelief. 'Not everyone realises that it is a way of life, not an add-on to a busy life.'

As I sit there uncomfortably in my high-kneed lotus position, it strikes me that I am a fraud among the fold. I am one of the 'some people'.

Outside in the thriving garden, I pull up weeds and cut back branches, as part of my work meditation. I should be focusing all of my attention on the actions of cutting and weeding, but the thoughts have won the battle here too. I am assailed by thoughts of the new house that Alastair and I had been planning to buy in Oxford. I am still adamant that I will take out a huge mortgage and buy the house: a final bid to keep my family from crumbling. *When I move to our new house in Oxford, I will plant a herb garden, maybe in that green area in the front, by the hedge. I will spend all my free time creating a rose garden in Alastair's honour. What kind of vegetables will I plant first? Maybe the herb garden should go in the top part of the garden, nearer the kitchen.* The thoughts whirr and buzz around my mind, no helium balloons in sight to even attempt to lasso them and send them on their way.

In the hallway of the old manor, I come across a statue of the Buddha, a lit candle and a round, painted stone. On the stone are three words: 'Be Here Now.' I find myself coming back to this stone again and again, rubbing its smoothness slowly and following the curves of the letters with my finger. 'Be Here Now,' I whisper to myself. My body is here, but my mind is far, far away. It is rooted in the past. It is hunched down, hiding out defensively with Alastair. An image appears repeatedly in my mind. Alastair is holding a bottle of wine and urging me to come and join him in a local B&B. The mind is stronger than the mindfulness. The past is stronger than the present.

After three days at the retreat, in the middle of a lengthy silent sitting meditation, I decide to leave. I can feel the excitement rising within me. I am breaking free. I stand up and leave the room, where the others continue in silent meditation. I half-walk, half-run up to my bedroom, throw my clothes into my backpack and take the sheets off the bed. I drop the sheets down to the laundry room and write a short message that I pin to the co-ordinator's door: 'Sorry I have to leave, but I am just not ready to deal with so much silence. Bébhinn.'

I walk briskly outside and wince at the brightness of the day. I open the car, throw my bag over to the passenger seat and jump in.

On the lawn, the other retreaters are now doing a silent walking meditation, looking more like sedated inmates of a mental health institution than seekers in search of peace of spirit. I let out a whoop as the car skids on the gravel, leaving behind the silent, focused steps of the retreaters and a few quizzical looks. In the car, I have one clear thought: I need to see the children. I need to be with them. I drive straight to the airport to catch a flight to Ireland.

'The best thing that came out of that retreat,' my father jokes later, 'is that you came back wanting to weed my garden.'

I think, in fact, that he is right.

Desperately seeking solutions III

The feeling of brokenness is overwhelming. The weekends in Wimbledon are unbearable. I cannot stay in the house. It has turned from a home to a lifeless building, a prison where the ghost of our former life as a family taunts me in every corner. I stay out of the house until the children's bedtime and we can all scurry upstairs and tumble straight into sleep. Sundays are the worst. Everywhere I go, I am bombarded by images of men carrying their toddlers on their shoulders or kicking a football with the kids in the park, while the mother sits reading a newspaper. Mother's time off. On these days, the double-seated pushchair feels particularly hard to manoeuvre on the cobblestone paths through the park and each creak of the pushchair seems to pant *Alastair – should – not – have – died.* Even the boys seem more whiny and demanding on Sundays.

When Alastair and I married, I told him that he was the man I wanted to be with not only in good moments, but the one I wanted by my side in any bad moments that life might throw at us too. Here I am drowning in the worst moment of my life, and he is nowhere to be found. I am twice cursed: once by Alastair's death, and again by not having him by my side to face it.

I am awash with unspent, futile love. All the attention and

care I gave to Alastair bubbles within me without release. I crave physical intimacy. I miss being held, being kissed. I long to scare away the spectre of death by making endless, mindless love. But with whom? Alastair's death has boosted my libido and reduced to zero my outlet. I confide this to my sister, laughing dryly. Who would have thought Alastair's death would make me feel like this? Maybe my heightened, almost paranoid awareness of death has intensified my animal urge to reproduce: *keep the DNA alive, keep the DNA alive.* My sister, always the practical one, responds by buying me a vibrator. I laugh outright when she gives it to me, forgetting myself and my despair for a moment. But the threatened animal is not so easily fooled – it is not pleasure it claws for, but survival.

One weekend I have a visit from one of Alastair's closest friends, J. On this visit, I realise that I can talk with him in a way reminiscent of the way I used to talk with Alastair. It dawns on me that he is the closest thing to Alastair left in the world. We play backgammon together, watch and re-watch DVDs with the kids, drink beer and reminisce about Brazil, where he had stayed with Alastair and me on many an occasion. He is my friend as well as Alastair's and he always loved Alastair fiercely and talked reverently about Alastair's and my relationship – the type of relationship he has not yet found.

He visits on a beautiful summer's Sunday and we decide to go to the fair in Wimbledon village. I strap Liam into the buggy, while Tom scrambles onto J's shoulders. We walk through our flower-dappled local park and for the first time in months I feel a relaxed and relieved peace in the early-morning family-feel of Sunday. Up in Wimbledon village, we put the children on merry-go-rounds, eat candyfloss and win little teddies for each of them. We have a competition to see who can find the tackiest item in the many stalls selling mostly cheap, plastic ornaments. We run around the fair, chasing the boys and laughing. An image of our last day with Alastair at the fair in Santa Cruz flashes through my mind, and I smile. When I need to go to the bathroom, I casually ask J to mind the children and I stroll leisurely off on my own. What a change from the usual need to saddle both unwilling and protesting boys into the buggy and push them across muddy grass to find a loo.

As I walk, I smile at all the families around me and am infused with the sweetest sense of relief. I have been given a day's reprieve from my grieving. Here we are a family again, sharing the boys and jokes between us, like every other family. J had mentioned that he has a sore throat and I go to the pharmacy and buy him some medicine, without him asking. I feel the joy of being able to take care of a man, of taking part again in the competition in generosity that characterised Alastair's and my marriage.

On the way back from the pharmacy, I see him pushing the two laughing boys on swings and I am suddenly struck by the depth of my relief and pleasure. In the middle of the muddy field, I start to cry. I want so desperately to be a part of a family again, to have a man to love, to share the children.

As the day wears on, I am gripped by the frightening thought that Alastair's friend will soon leave, taking with him these feelings and leaving me once again with the sense of clawing desperation and loneliness. That evening, over a beer and game of backgammon, I broach the idea of him staying on, tentatively suggesting at the possibility of starting a relationship. He sips his beer and thoughtfully moves his backgammon pieces.

'I'm not sure that's going to work,' he drawls slowly, not taking his eyes off the board.

I feel the bitter slap of embarrassment and budding anger rise in my cheeks. 'I'm really vulnerable at the moment,' I say tightly, trying to sound casual, 'I don't know if I can quite take rejection.'

'Exactly,' he says, looking me in the eyes. 'You are really vulnerable at the moment.'

He leaves the next day, hugging the boys and me tightly before he goes.

Survival guilt

I am sinking in a pool of guilt.

I feel guilty that I would even think of having a relationship with anybody other than Alastair. I try to reason with myself, reminding myself that I had no feelings for J before Alastair died, that I loved Alastair so totally and so recently. But my desperation has a stronger pull than reason.

I feel a strong guilt about Alastair's death too. Guilty that I had not understood that he was going to die, nor been present and together enough to ease him through it. Guilty that I did not understand that he was telling me he loved me before he lost consciousness. Guilty that I was not there at the moment he stopped breathing. I even feel guilty for believing that he is dead. Others can be duped, but for me to admit he has died feels like the ultimate betrayal.

I feel guilty that I did not kneel in the hospital corridor and scream and scream until someone made him better.

I feel guilty too for contributing to his death. That year, Alastair had been preparing for a tough promotion. He was working long hours and travelling a lot. He had been under the weather, with a knee operation the year before and an unshakeable bug a few months before he died. There were signs that his body was under stress. At the same time, I had started my full-time job and was annoyed that I always had to clock off at five o'clock to get back in time to relieve the nanny, while Alastair worked until late. I was feeling frustrated that the responsibility of the children still fell mostly to me, even though I too was working full-time. I let Alastair know just how I felt.

On top of his work, Alastair was spending time looking for a family home and a school for Tom in Oxford with all the due diligence he put into everything. He was still coming home too at three thirty on Friday afternoons to bring Tom to his soccer class. I suspect that all this work, stress and family pressures had weakened Alastair's immune system. I cannot find any other explanation why such a healthy, young man would suddenly die from a relatively innocuous and commonplace bacterium. In light of his death, I start to question why I had not supported him through his efforts for promotion, staying at home with the children, taking on the tasks of finding a home and a school in Oxford, meeting him with a relaxed, welcoming home when he came back from work, rather than being on the computer finishing off my work, irritated and tired after putting the children to bed.

All of the ways I fell short of the perfect Stepford wife flash through my mind and I feel the weight of my own ego in our relationship. Perhaps if he was still alive, this would be the normal tug-of-war of a reciprocal, negotiated relationship. In the aftermath of his death, however, it shakes me to the core and makes me question all of my demands on Alastair and on our relationship.

In August, Alastair's mother and I are sitting in my stationary car in a Sainsbury's car park when I quietly admit my sense of guilt to her. It is a feeling I have been guarding closely during these three long months, a shame I am afraid to let others see.

'Oh,' she says, in the most offhand, casual way, 'I felt so guilty too, and I have talked to so many widows over the years and each one feels guilty at the death of her husband.'

I sigh deeply and watch her words weave magic on me.

Her words, her casual tone, allow me to glimpse how natural my feelings are. To the backdrop of car bumpers and wayward trolleys, I lean over the gear stick and hug her tightly. Seeing this sense of guilt as part of the process of grieving makes me doubt the veracity of my own guilt. Alastair's mother plants a seed of doubt in my choking conviction, which allows other explanations space to enter. I glimpse the interminable road of 'what-ifs' and realise it is a dead-end alley.

Perhaps the world does not move around my axis. Perhaps I did not bring on Alastair's death or fail to save him. Our relationship was loving and alive. We were not preparing for death nor living in its shadow. We imagined we had a full lifetime together and we were still testing and working out the terms of our relationship.

The seed of doubt enables me to go a bit easier on myself. I loved him as best I could and he loved me back. I gave him what he most wanted in life: a real, loving, laughter-filled relationship and two edible sons. I was by his side in his last conscious hours.

Perhaps I was enough. I exhale in a deep, relieving sigh, one tiny layer of suffering shed.

Escaping the ghosts

Each time one of my desperate attempts at finding a solution to Alastair's death fails, I return to my last shred of hope. *I will be ok when I get to Oxford. I will be ok when I get to Oxford.*

I begin to prepare for our move, sifting through the debris of our family home, trying to work out what to take with us, what to put in storage and what must now be thrown away. I start by emptying out the drawers in our bedroom. In the first drawer, I come across an old birthday card from Alastair. It throws me. I sit tracing my finger over the words 'My Love' for two hours before I can move on to the next item. I fill an old suitcase to the brim with Alastair's clothes and heave it to a local charity shop. I hand over the suitcase and run. The idea of emptying Alastair's clothes onto the floor of the charity shop or watching a picky octogenarian judge the quality of his endless shirts makes my stomach churn. It takes weeks to empty the whole house, and all the while I am convincing myself that I am only *lending* our piano and our bed to my friends, that I can have our red chenille sofa back *whenever I want*.

I go with a friend and Alastair's sister to visit the outside of the house that Alastair and I had planned to buy in Oxford. The family has already moved out. I am prepared to sink all of our money into buying the house. I cling to it as the last home that he and I will ever choose together. It represents our future, our family home. I remember Alastair's romanticism of Fairfields, the family home that his mother sold shortly after his father died, when he was five. I am adamant not to rob my boys of their family home. Perhaps if I buy the house, then our family will have some structure again. I consider whether it is better to sell the house in London or keep it and rent it out while negotiating a hefty mortgage for the house in Oxford. I walk my friend and Alastair's sister around the three lawns of the house and tell them what I imagined for each lawn while on my Buddhist retreat. 'Here is where I will put the herb garden,' I point out, 'and over here is where I will put the vegetable patch.' We walk through the kitchen and dining room together. 'The whole downstairs needs to be redone,' I tell them, 'but that is something to keep me busy.'

My friend hugs me. 'You're so brave,' she whispers.

Alastair's sister bites her lip. 'Don't you think this is taking on too much?' she asks gently.

I mull over her question for a couple of weeks. I talk to our bank manager. I look out on our tiny badly shorn lawn in London. I stop to listen to the exhaustion I feel when I have to change a lightbulb.

In August, I find myself on the front porch of this new house in Oxford, desolately crying over another nugget of loss as I accept that I cannot buy it. The last thing I need is a big mortgage hanging over us. I will not be earning in the next four years while I am studying, so I need the rental income from the house in London to maintain the boys and me. The scholarships I have applied for do not offer enough to support two young children. Both options – getting a big mortgage, or selling the house in London – are out of the question. When was it that practicality fell so far out of alignment with romanticism?

Instead of buying the house, I move in September to a rented, picturesque butler's house on the grounds of Wytham Manor. I notice with relief that it has no lawn to mow, but instead a paved courtyard where the children can play. Wytham is a tiny village, about three kilometres outside of Oxford, with a comfortable pub, a small but well-stocked shop, a welcoming chapel and an endless, wild bluebell wood beckoning us. Our landlord tells us that the wood is full of badger hides and owl nests. 'Deep in the middle of the forest,' he tells a wide-eyed Tom, 'there is a tree that is over two thousand years old.'

The whole village seems to have been created to harbour us during this year after Alastair's death. The community is small and inclusive. When I meet one of the mothers in the village playground, she invites me to the harvest supper that will be held in the community hall. When I stop to introduce myself to another neighbour, he invites me to play Aunt Sally, which turns out to be an old English throwing game, outside the pub on Tuesday evenings.

The house is made of grey stone and has pink roses growing along its façade. It has three bedrooms, a good-sized living room and a cosy kitchen. It is the perfect nest for us. About twenty metres in front of our main door, there is a low, rounded archway. Again and again, and again, I imagine Alastair coming through that archway at the end of a day's work, his suit flapping at his side as he hurries briskly home. He has to bend his head to avoid hitting it against the stone.

He is framed there, under the archway, night after night, but he never moves beyond it.

Oxford blues

Of all of us, Tom adapts best to Oxford. He loves his school and makes friends easily. In the morning, he is always the one to wake me up. He shakes me awake and I fall back into the pillows and tell him to dress himself. He comes back dressed and I tell him to go and eat his breakfast and give breakfast to his two-year-old brother. He comes back having eaten and fed his brother. At this stage, I feel enough pity for this sweet, anxious boy to get out of bed and drive him to school.

One day, as I pick him up from school, his teacher comes close and whispers something to me. At first I do not catch what she says and ask her to repeat it. 'His pyjamas are in his bag,' she says.

With embarrassment, I peer into his little school bag and sure enough, there are his pyjamas neatly folded. This little four-year-old boy had dressed himself over his pyjamas that morning, while his mother tried to block life out with numbing sleep.

Tom is articulate about the suffering in the house. 'Are you crying about Daddy again?' he asks, annoyed, as I slump against the oven in tears.

Tom asks endless questions about death, about where his daddy is, about what his daddy was like. I answer as honestly and simply as I can. For me, it feels like his daddy is off on some long trip and I am adamant to keep him as present as possible. For Tom's first day at school in Oxford, we draw pictures for Daddy to tell him all about it. On that first morning before school, Tom stands smiling in our stone courtyard, lost and lovely in his new school uniform, and ties the picture messages onto the strings of four helium balloons. He then lets them go with a whoop and they dip and soar into the air towards Daddy in the sky. We light candle after candle on special days to have Daddy present. By day, as we play chasing games among the snowdrops and bluebells of the local forest, I tell him that each butterfly that crosses our path is Daddy keeping close to us. At night, we seek out the brightest star and I tell him that it is his daddy, shining down on him.

Tom asks me why his daddy died and why other children still have their daddies. I have no answer to give him and I share his sense of injustice. I tell him it is a mystery, but that for some reason Daddy has to be in heaven now and we have to continue here without him. 'You had the most loving daddy for three years,' I tell him. 'Some children never have a loving daddy.'

I try to diminish the sense of injustice and minimise a sense of victimhood, but it rings hollow.

'How did Daddy die?' he asks me.

'A bug went into his body and made him die,' I tell him gently.

'Where did the bug come from?'

'It was in the air, maybe in the aeroplane or somewhere like that. Bugs are all around us and most are harmless.'

'Will a bug get into my body?' he asks apprehensively.

I assure him and reassure him that he is going to be fine, but he starts to wash his hands compulsively and refuses to share cups or water bottles with anyone, even family. I sigh, chiding myself for having somehow said the wrong thing.

Tom asks if I will die too. I hug him close to me and reassure him that no, it is very unlikely that I will die before he is all grown up.

'But what if you do, Mummy?' he insists.

'If I die,' I reassure him, 'you have so many other people to take care of you.'

We sit on his bed and draw our family tree, which shows endless grandparents, uncles and aunts. He snuggles close to me, satisfied. 'Can I watch more TV if you die?' he asks impishly, making me smile. I tickle him into full belly laughter.

Liam is younger, unable to articulate his distress and confusion and he seems to suffer more from the changes. He screams and wails each morning when I leave him at nursery school. I stand at the wall of the nursery, out of sight, and cry until he quietens down. I start each morning in this way and then go into Oxford to escape into a bubble of research and learning. Liam is sleeping less and less at night and wakes with terrible screaming tantrums. His attitude towards me swings dramatically, from clinging to me desperately to railing his mighty fury against me. I am exhausted by him. My attitude swings wildly too, from feeling anger towards him for making my life so difficult at a time that I am so unable to deal with it, to feeling overwhelmed with pity and love for my poor, fatherless baby. We are locked in mutual despair: this little boy manifesting the unhappiness of our whole home.

I dive desperately into life in Oxford, starting lectures and tutorials on social policy and child development, meeting with my supportive advisor and defining my research question. All the while, I hungrily seek information about outcomes for children who have lost their fathers. In general, how do they do in education, in mental health, in their general behaviour? Relieved, I learn that only a slightly higher number of children who lose their fathers have bad outcomes, compared to those in stable, two-parent families. Fathers, it reassures me, are the icing on the cake for children, but the mother is the cake itself.

Language gangs up on me as I make new acquaintances. The pronouns kill me. I keep referring to our children and stumble back to *my* children. When people ask me benign questions about my husband, I trip over what tense to use. 'He is English, not Irish' or 'he was English, not Irish?' I resolve to say, 'I married an Englishman', safe to give an honest answer without having to refer to his death. When I finally have to tell people that he has died, it aches to say the brutal words: 'My husband died.' It conjures up images of Alastair lying on the hospital bed and leaves me breathless with dismay. 'I am a widow,' I finally admit when the conversation is becoming too tricky. Later, as I begin to refer to Alastair, language once again trips me up. Is he my *ex-husband*? No, there has been no break-up; he still feels like my husband. My *dead husband*? Too direct. I finally settle on *late husband*, enjoying the joke with Alastair each time I say it, as he was indeed always late for everything in life.

I apply for two scholarships for my PhD. It takes such extraordinary effort to focus my mind on the applications and the subsequent interviews. I have never failed to win a scholarship before in my academic career, but this time, when my life is at rock bottom, I am refused for both. The disappointment and unfamiliar sense of academic failure are hard to swallow. What is life doing? Before, when I was stronger and more able to cope with knock-backs, I had sailed through life, and now life is kicking me when I am down. Why is life closing doors on me? If Alastair had been here, he would have helped me. If Alastair had been here, I could have done better.

Alastair should not have died; he should not have died.

No easy answers

During our first week in Oxford, I register the boys and myself at the local doctor's office in nearby Wolvercote. I explain our situation to the doctor and inform him of Alastair's death four months earlier.

'You know that you won't feel 'normal' for at least two years?' he states bluntly.

I balk at the idea of feeling as I do for two years.

'Would you like me to see if I can set up some counselling for you?' he asks helpfully.

I nod emphatically.

Shortly after Alastair's death, I had sat on the edge of my bed in Wimbledon, ringing around charities and counselling services for support on how to help the boys deal with their father's death. In the wardrobe mirror, I saw my reflection hunched over the phone, clinging to it in the hope of finding a way to erase the scar that their father's death will leave on their lives. The wardrobe door gaped open slightly, showing a dangling sleeve of one of Alastair's shirts.

I want in any way possible to protect the boys from such a start in life. They are promising racehorses, faltering only moments after leaving the gate.

Everywhere I rang told me that they only support children aged five and upwards and suggested that I get back in touch in a couple of years' time. Finally, one woman, hearing the desperation in my voice, gave me some motherly advice. 'The best thing you can do for children so young is for you to be ok. Happy mother: happy children.'

This is just the green light I need. Before Alastair's death, I had never received any counselling or psychotherapy. Not necessarily because I did not need it, but because I had an unarticulated belief, shared perhaps by most people I know in just-get-on-with-it Ireland, that counselling is for the weak or self-obsessed, those who have some form of mental illness or instability and need to be cured. I also harboured the belief that people who attend counselling do not have good friends, with whom they can talk honestly and openly about their lives.

Alastair's death has freed me from my own limited understanding of counselling. Everybody around me is loving and supportive, but nobody can help me find any peace or understanding in my own head about Alastair's death. I do not even want to share some of my thoughts, so as not to provoke more suffering in others or to give them an opportunity to judge me as anything but the heartbroken, loyal and loving widow. I need a filter to help me articulate and analyse the thoughts that are arising in the incessant chatter of my mind, before I can even begin to discuss them with my closest friends, my family or my mother-in-law.

Therefore, when the doctor in Wolvercote suggests counselling, I jump at the opportunity. On the following Wednesday evening, I peel Liam off my leg, give a hopeful smile to a nervous babysitter and drive through heavy rain to a small, sparse NHS clinic, which is hidden among a row of shops. The counsellor is a comfortably dressed man in his forties, wearing small, rimmed glasses and a warm smile. He invites me to sit down. I sit in a torn, leather chair amongst the medical equipment and begin to tell my tale. Over the hour, I am transported from the grotty NHS clinic to the scenes of my life with Alastair. I can almost smell the newly cut grass of the park where we first kissed and the Brazilian coffee of our lazy Sunday mornings.

For three months Wednesday evenings become the highlight of my week. I let everything tumble out of me. I cry desolately with the new luxury of being in the company of someone who does not try to cheer me up. Here I am again with an intelligent, funny, self-effacing Englishman to share my inner thoughts. He listens with infinite patience as I sing my song of despair to him: *Alastair should not have died. He should not have died.* I wince, then smile, as my counsellor volleys back my inconsistencies and sloppy, indulgent thinking. I beg him to give me the ten easy steps to feeling better, but he holds up his empty hands in the air before me with a friendly 'sorry'.

'Don't you get it yet?' he asks me gently.

'Get what?' I ask.

'No one can show you the way out of this but you, yourself.'

One evening, when life is black for me, he mentions antidepressants. The suggestion jolts me into wakefulness. I do not want to sedate my way out of sadness. I do not want a recipe to merely function enough in society to avoid bothering those around me. I long to recognise myself again. I long to laugh again. Really laugh.

The counselling has pricked holes in my idealisation of my life before Alastair's death. I see now that there were moments of uncertainty and a low hum of dissatisfaction with my life, even then. When Alastair died, I had been keeping a notepad by my bed and each night before I went to sleep I wrote down three things I was grateful for that day. I had done this to dispel the feeling of incompletion that I was experiencing, despite a happy family life.

I am slowly becoming aware of the wake-up call that Alastair's death is for me and of the light it is shining on all those questions that have whirred, often unconsciously, within me. *What is life? Why am I alive? What remains of us after death? What should I do with my limited time on earth?* Lifelong questions awaken within me, freed from the anaesthetic of everyday busyness and my own unconscious denial of my mortality.

I do want to stop feeling dreadful, and, beyond that, I want to learn everything there is to learn from the rip that Alastair's death has torn into the illusion of my life.

Pleasure and pain

I am drawn to graveyards. On afternoons after picking Tom and Liam up from school, I walk around old graveyards with them and read tombstone after tombstone. When I see a tombstone of someone who died younger than Alastair, I feel a sense of relief. Alastair was luckier than *that* person. And *that* person. I do not want Alastair to be demoted to 'poor Alastair'. I want to believe he is loved by God, favoured by life. I am half-waiting for some tragedy, some nuclear explosion to occur so that I can know, 'That's why Alastair died. He was a good man, a beautiful man. Alastair should have died. He should have died to be spared from *this*.'

On many tombstones, I read the dates of couples who were reunited in death. Many of those who died in old age seem to die soon after one another. As if one could not live long without the other. Others have dates of twenty or thirty years apart before they were reunited. How long will it take for me to be reunited with Alastair? The Indian custom of the widow throwing herself on the funeral pyre makes some small sense to me now. There is a period after Alastair dies when I die too. It is a period of crisis: the old life has ended and there is no new life arising from the ashes. Is it true that a new life will arise?

In quiet moments, I allow myself to cry and marvel as the grief rips through me. Slumped against the kitchen counter as the boys eat their meal or in the evening when they have both fallen asleep at last, I let grief have its way with me. I am more an object than the subject of this grief. The grief is bigger than I am and I bow to it. What comes out of my mouth is more of a cough than a cry: something needs to be released from within me. I am dismayed by the lack of linearity in grieving. I had imagined that the grief would get easier to deal with over time, day by day it would be diluted. But grief is not linear; it comes in waves. The scripted stages – from denial, anger, bargaining, depression to acceptance – co-exist in time. They are not played out in some linear perfection. Some days the grief is lighter and I feel a sense of distance and progress. On other days, I am swallowed whole by the monster of grief and stand weeping, my emotions naked to two uncomprehending children.

When this happens, I paraphrase one of Tom's favourite night-time stories again and again. There is no going over the grief, nor under it and certainly not around it. Oh no, I whisper to myself, I've got to go through it!

A friend tells me that her cousin, who is still single, proclaimed on hearing of Alastair's death: 'But how is it that I haven't even started my story and her story is already over?' This plays on my mind. My story is already over. How quick it has been, how short the time between newlywed and widow. How quickly I moved from planning to reminiscing. How old I feel. How suddenly age has pounced on me. At times, I look in the mirror and cannot believe that this young face is mine. Like Dorian Gray, I am not what I seem. Within me, there is a hidden portrait of my real self, wrinkled, worn and weary.

With the help of my counsellor, I begin to see the pain I am feeling as the price I pay for the love I shared with Alastair in the seven years we were together. Despite the sharpness of the loss, which often leaves me panting for breath or reaching for a second bottle of wine, I know that I would not have missed one moment of my time with him to avoid the pain I now feel. If the non-negotiable price of the memories of my life with Alastair is this pain, then I grudgingly accept it and stop fighting so mercilessly against it.

In moments, there is however a solace in the grief I feel. It keeps the link between Alastair and me vividly alive and I offer it to him as the price I am prepared to pay for the love and adventures we shared. Being locked in grief keeps us together. I hold on desperately to the life we had, to the dreams we shared. I continue to be his wife. He continues to be the father of our children. We are a family of four and the world is our oyster. Each moment of suffering is the friction between how life was and how life is. If I was to let go of this friction, I might lose him. If I let go of this friction, I might lose myself.

When Alastair's best friend G asks me how I am, I stoically tell him that I am taking the pain as the flipside of all the moments of love we shared. 'Surely the pain must feel so close and those moments so distant now?' he retorts.

I smile and shake my head, but say nothing. It's only by going through it that you understand that the remnants of the pleasure are somehow alive in the pain.

Grace

It is early October and I am driving to Tom's school to pick him up. It is a bright, crisp day and the sunlight plays on my eyes as I drive. The straight road ahead is tightly lined on each side with thick, dark-green pine trees and it seems to rise up before me, thinning out to the horizon. I pass the house that Alastair and I were going to buy, as I do twice each day dropping Tom off and again in the afternoon when I pick him up. Once again, I imagine myself driving in. Alastair is sitting on the porch and stands up to welcome me. He seems so natural as he moves towards me. He seems older, quieter. As he reaches for the handle of the car door, I shake myself out of the daydream. My mind is sagging now under the weight of my sadness and suffering.

Suddenly, from the ashes of sorrow, a quiet elation rises and washes over me and my soul sings. My body is weightless and I have the stomach-churning feeling that the car and I are floating above the road, rising to the treetops. I do not want to breathe in case the bubble in my chest bursts. My mind stills; the mild afternoon air echoes through it.

One word forms, visible before me. The word is Grace.

Slowly, the sensation passes and I continue down the road, the indicator breaking the silence abruptly as I turn into Tom's school.

Fifth wedding anniversary

The first of everything is an echoing of the loss of Alastair. Tom's first birthday after he died is overshadowed by memories of Alastair joking with the children in the garden at his last birthday. Liam's first birthday after Alastair's death is overshadowed by the fact that Alastair had only lived for one of Liam's birthday celebrations. Our first wedding anniversary after he died was to be our fifth, and falls five months after he died. I decide to bring the boys down to the little house in Wales that belongs to Alastair's mother.

I am dreading the day of the anniversary. The boys and I set out on our favourite walk to Pobbles Beach, a walk that Alastair and I have often undertaken hand in hand, with Liam in a sling or on Alastair's shoulders and Tom scrambling ahead of us. Now I try to cajole the boys along the sandy dunes, but end up trudging along slowly, carrying both of them. *Alastair should not have died. He should be here. I need him here.*

The day is bright, windy and dry. The crashing waves on the beach and the looming grassy cliffs are food to a hungry soul. I was worried that I would feel alone and unhappy on this day, but as I walk I feel an enormous peace. Throughout the day, I am flooded by a memory that takes all thoughts of sadness and despair away. About six months before he died, Alastair went to Russia on business. We had previously promised each other that we would explore Russia together. I had been putting the children to sleep when he called to say, with a laugh in his voice, that he had arrived in Russia and was in the taxi on the way to the hotel. 'I have my eyes completely shut,' he said playfully, 'I won't see one bit of Russia without you, except for the hotel and meeting room.' I laughed and put the boys on the phone to say their goodnights to him and I asked him to call me later.

Just as the boys went to sleep, the phone rang again. I sat on the top stair of the landing. Alastair's voice was quieter, more peaceful now. 'I am in the hotel,' he said, 'and the room overlooks Red Square. The square is covered in a blanket of hushed snow and it is gently snowing. It's spectacular,' he said, in a near whisper. 'And all I can think is that I wish you were here to share it with me.'

Out of nowhere, this memory comes to me again and again on our wedding anniversary. Each time my mind moves towards a thought of sadness or awareness of Alastair's absence, this memory comes to my mind.

I fall asleep on the day of our fifth wedding anniversary with the sound of Alastair's calming voice ringing in my ears, reassuring me that wherever he is, it is spectacular and he wishes I was there to share it with him.

Fortieth

Early December brings with it Alastair's fortieth birthday, which weighs heavily on my thoughts. When I had bemoaned Alastair's long hours and his lack of deep satisfaction at work, he would reassure me, saying, 'I promise you, Bébhinn, I will be doing something different at forty.'

Now his birthday is days away, and he has been dead six months. I have to give it to him. He is certainly doing something different, but it aches that the change was so drastic and tragic.

I invite his mother and some of his friends to dinner in my sister's house in London to celebrate his birthday. I spend the morning preparing Alastair's signature dishes: chicken and leek pie and his *pièce de resistance*, chocolate cheesecake. As I cook, I remember the first time we celebrated a birthday together. It was my twenty-fifth birthday and Alastair came around and cooked this same meal for me and my friends and family in my flat in London. He set up a table and added the ironing board to give more length. 'We'll cover it with a cloth and no one will even notice,' he had laughed.

I have never cooked a full meal for Alastair's friends, usually being sous-chef to Alastair at most parties. As I prepare and cook the food, I do it with all my love for him and the morning passes in a meditative peace. When his friends arrive, we have a delicious meal to the sound of the laughter of Alastair's two sons, as they play with his friends' children. The conversation is easy and flowing. Alastair's presence is light and loving.

Every cell of me is awake to the fact that I am alone. I watch the couples as they dance unconsciously. He sees her empty wine glass and fills it. She separates some wing meat and passes it to him. He makes her tea with milk and one sugar, just as she likes it. I, too, am well looked after; everyone is very kind to the new widow, but they ask: 'Would you like more wine? Breast or leg? How do you like your tea?' I belong to no one.

That night, I fall exhausted into bed. As I lie, marvelling at having survived the day, I am suddenly assailed by a vivid image of our last skiing trip. Alastair is before me in his orange ski jacket and his open ski boots. He is smiling and, as always, he is carrying my skis as well as his own. Whenever we skied, he would wordlessly take my skis from me and lift them over his second shoulder. It was one of the many gestures of love that he showered on me.

This gentle image of love is my undoing. I curl into a ball in the bed in utter despair, desperately missing this unequalled friend and minder of me.

First Christmas

The days are getting colder and I recoil into myself, desperate to escape the winter of my discontent. The first Christmas without Alastair approaches. The idea of buying the children's presents alone and being a lone Father Christmas to them fills me with emptiness. I dread the forced joviality of a Christmas dinner, where I am the only one without a partner by my side. I cannot bear to put on a paper hat, pull the Christmas crackers and share their lame jokes in a grand pretence of celebration. Christmas only accentuates Alastair's absence. Everywhere, the Christmas song 'Fairytale of New York' jeers me: *'Can't make it all alone, I built my dreams around you.'*

The date strides towards me mercilessly. I want to skip it, maybe volunteer for a soup kitchen or join others to raise awareness for homelessness by taking part in a twenty-four hour fast and sleeping rough on Christmas Eve night. I am looking for ways to dodge the day.

Out of nowhere, this dread begins to loosen its grip on me. A wind of peace blows within me, untangling the knot in my stomach. I am filled with a serene happiness and, in the depths of my soul, I know: Alastair has found peace. The knowledge settles within me and I am awash with gratitude and love. For the first five months after his death, I sensed that Alastair was unsettled, that his soul was shocked and confused by what had happened. After five months, at our wedding anniversary, I understood that he was more peaceful, beginning to appreciate the beauty of where he was, but still attached to all of us in life. I do not know if this is a projection of my own emotions, but it calms me to believe it is him.

It is the twenty-third of December and I am making a collage of photos of Alastair and the boys to hang beside the Christmas tree. In the centre of the collage, I paste these words in big letters: 'All is well; Al is well.' On the same day, I receive an email from Alastair's friend J. He has had his first post-death dream of Alastair, and Alastair was radiantly happy and joking. He woke up feeling a strong sense of peace.

The sensation of Alastair's well-being frees me to participate in Christmas with a genuine happiness at being with my family. It dawns on me that this Christmas could be my last with any one of my other family members, including my children. I remember that loss is not doled out in fair and even portions. Having lost once does not protect me from losing other people in my life. What if my dad dies next year and I didn't spend his last Christmas with him?

Alastair's death reminds me that I can lose anyone at any time. His death reminds me that there are no guarantees of having more time with the people I love. I have got to grab the opportunities that are before me. To the boys' delight, I fly with them to Ireland, to spend Christmas in the embrace of my parents' home. The cacophony of cousins fills each nook and cranny of the day, which scuttles past like any other.

Death is teaching me to appreciate life. The dead are teaching me to appreciate the living.

Making time to grieve

The boys stay on with my family for a week in Ireland, as I return to Oxford to catch up on my research for the PhD. Early in the New Year, I sit in the stony-cold house in Oxford and look out at the frozen courtyard. The changing of the year has been a relief to me. I tell myself, 'My husband died *last* year.' I tell new people I meet, 'My husband died *last* year.' As if the tragedy has passed. As if it is not so shocking. As if his death is farther from me now.

I have not made much headway on my research or reading, and my mother is arriving tomorrow with the boys. The idea of the boys' arrival fills me with both relief and dread. How I have missed them during this week. But how can I do all my reading with them demanding so much of my time and emotional energy?

I have been in Oxford for over four months, but I am not as ok as I had hoped. It has taken me more than six months to realise that the next move will not make it better; I will not be ok next week, or after the first year. Alastair's death has flipped my life upside-down, externally and internally, and I will have to change with it. I cannot live a shadow of my former life, pretending that soon I will be able to continue as before.

I am walking the thin, desperate line between coping and breakdown. 'Something has got to give,' I whisper to myself. 'Something has simply got to give.'

It is clear to me now that I have to face Alastair's death. It is an imperative. I have tried to get on with my life but 'stiff upper lip' is not the path for me. I have to stop and open up to what has happened and dedicate my time and energy to working through it. This is the only way I can be whole again. The idea of being separated any longer from the boys is abhorrent to me. It is difficult with them, but it is unbearable without them.

That leaves the PhD. My PhD can go on hold, I think to myself. Maybe I will start again in a year's time or when I am more peaceful, more accepting. This is a time when the boys need me and I need them. A PhD can wait. They, however, cannot. I ring my supportive supervisor and she accepts my decision graciously.

When the boys arrive from Ireland the next day, I am fully present to receive them.

Keeping Alastair close I

The days loom long before me, now that I am not working or studying. 'What do I do now?' I ask Alastair's friend J desperately. 'What do I do now?'

'Find out what makes you happy,' he suggests, 'and do as much of it as you can.'

Being close to Alastair makes me happy. Keeping him at the centre of my life is all that I want to do. I begin with the box full of condolence cards and letters that I had received after his death. I read each one again. Each letter seems brand new to me, as if my memory is desperately deleting all reference to the time around Alastair's death. I search for religious remembrance or thank you cards to send in return to each person. My googling shows me only old-fashioned, bible-laced offerings. Instead of a remembrance card, I design a simple card with a photo of Alastair at the top of the mountain on our recent skiing trip, grinning widely and raising a full pint of beer at the camera. In gold-coloured ink below the photo, I print: 'Alastair Ramsay on top of the world.' I spend time on each thank you card I write, remembering every kind act and word. I am reliving the support of our wide circle of family, friends and work colleagues again, and once again their gestures of love and concern flood me with a sense of calm.

When a colleague of Alastair's approaches me about compiling a short film about Alastair's life, I jump at the chance. After the boys have gone to bed, I open a second bottle of wine, turn on Brazilian bossa nova and sing our songs as I collect together all of the family video footage and go through the endless photos that we have of Alastair from birth to his last days. I talk to him out loud about how we will structure the film and who we will include to talk about him.

This gives me the perfect excuse to bring Alastair's close friends and family together and to record them as they tell stories of his life. I need his friends and family to help me conjure him to life again. Alastair is most present when I have others with whom to reminisce.

I tell myself that I am making the film for the boys. In part, this is true. Alastair lost his father as a boy and I witnessed Alastair's unquenchable thirst to know him. His father was the missing character in the theatre of his life and became a magnet for vague projections and unanswered questions. Many times, when we were playing or travelling with the boys, Alastair would stop in melancholic wonder. 'It's incredible that they won't remember any of this,' he would say. In these moments, he was realising how many times his own father must have played with him and he was disappointed that he had no concrete memories of those times.

'No,' I said, drawing from my limited knowledge of early childhood development, 'they won't remember what actually happened, but they will remember that they were loved. It will be in the way they grow up.'

Subconscious memories of Alastair do exist within Tom and Liam but they have almost no conscious memories that they can visit in quiet moments like old photographs. I ache with sadness when I remember that the boys will not know Alastair; his quirky sense of humour, his caring nature, the way he always left sun cream in his ears and pulled his sleeves over his hands.

Mostly though, the film is for me. Making it is an extension of our life together, a reprieve from the clawing sense of separation. I want to capture Alastair's essence, before time erodes the vividness of our memories. I want to offer both the boys and Alastair a bridge to each other. I want to keep our family together. Maybe too I will make a life-size cardboard cut-out of Alastair and put it in the kitchen. Life could go on pretty much as it was, I assure myself, with Alastair simply more silent than before.

'Daddy's video', when it is finished, is a jewel. It captures his laugh, the way he flips a pancake, his concentrated look as he eats an ice-cream and the looks of love he lavishes on me and on the boys. For months, it is my reward for surviving another day as one of the walking wounded in an oblivious world. It is also a chink through which the boys can spy their father. The boys sit on either side of me as I replay the film over and over to them. The opening scene is of Alastair, who was afraid of heights, doing a bungee jump. His face is chalk-white and his legs are trembling. 'But he did it anyway,' I whisper to the children, hugging them close. 'He was scared and he did it anyway.'

As we make new friends, the film becomes a way of introducing Alastair to them, of sharing with them a taste of this lovely man, who is an eternal member of our family.

Keeping Alastair close II

Alastair's friends in San Francisco, including all those who were with me at the time of his death, invite us back for a memorial hike in Alastair's honour in the awe-inducing oasis of Yosemite Park. One part of me shudders at the idea of returning to San

Francisco, but the stronger part of me rejoices. The trip is a bid to keep Alastair alive for me and for his friends.

In April, the boys and I brave another long flight from London, arriving jetlagged once again in San Francisco. I drag the tired boys to the car rental desk and they ask me what kind of car I want. Alastair used to drive around in an old Mustang convertible when he lived in San Francisco and I ask them if they have any available. Half an hour later, the boys and I are climbing the hills of San Francisco in a blue Mustang convertible, dazed with jetlag. From the back of the car, the boys whoop with delight as the wind whips their hair and we career down the wrong side of the road. My heart soars; San Francisco will not beat us.

We drive to Yosemite and meet with a large group of friends. The snow-capped mountains rise up above us and the fertility of nature buzzes audibly about us. On the first evening, we each paint a small stone with a message of love for Alastair, which we carry on our eight-mile hike to Kibbie Lake the next morning. As we wind our way through breathtaking gorges, Alastair's friends valiantly carry Tom and Liam on their shoulders. The boys see their first rattlesnake and point out the wild deer, as we clamber along rocks, push through charcoaled forests and wade over streams. We meet no other hikers on the path. The boys are the kings of the whole park. All the while, we share stories of Alastair.

I turn a corner and gasp sharply at the sight of Kibbie Lake. It is a breathlessly still expanse, a painted canvas laid out before me. Everyone digs into their backpacks and takes out the stones with the messages for Alastair and we make a circle with them.

This is an American Indian custom that we have borrowed for the day's ceremony. The circle is a space of love for Alastair's soul. We do not close the circle fully, but leave a gap so that his soul can move in and out of this circle of love for him.

Alastair's friends and I swim out into the middle of the lake, each with a little pinch of his ashes. Wishing him peace and well-being, each of us scatters a part of his ashes on the lake, his heyday at Stanford immortalised in the silver sparkle of the water. The tiny fish in the lake begin to bite and we drag ourselves out, mixing laughter and tears in another goodbye to Alastair.

After the hike, Alastair's friend L invites me to visit a well-respected spiritual healer and medium in the neighbouring state of Marin. I jump at the chance, desperate for some communication with Alastair.

The next day, I lie on the hard massage bed in the healer's room as she passes her hands over me.

'Alastair is more accepting now,' she reassures me with her eyes closed. 'He knew he would go before you, but is frustrated that it was so soon.' I breathe deeply, trying to connect with what she is telling me. 'Alastair frees you from your commitment to him,' she continues. 'You are free to be with another man. He doesn't free you from your commitment to raise his children though.'

I feel a bolt of anger rise from the pit of my stomach. I am suddenly fuming with anger towards Alastair.

'Who are you to free me from our commitment?' I flash at the healer, as if she were manifesting Alastair through her body. I sit up on the massage bed and start to shout at her, 'You left me, remember, you were the one who left me. You don't have the right to free me. It was until death do us part and death parted us, Alastair. I decide when I move on, not you.'

The sharpness of my anger takes me aback. It is like a lightning bolt striking out at the unperturbed healer. And then I start to cry. There is a knot of relief in my crying. Feeling anger at him breathes life back into our relationship, which is slipping mercilessly away through my fingers.

For one brief moment, we are together again in the battle of egos.

Keeping Alastair close III

We return to Oxford from San Francisco and are soon on the move again. Being in motion, I am finding, is lighter than being stationary. It is a perpetual, desperate movement towards Alastair, as if I might find him again in some other place. To mark the one-year anniversary of his death, his mother, the boys and I take a trip to Kirdcudbright in southern Scotland, where Alastair's father was born and bred. Because of his father's early death, Alastair never got to know his Scottish roots and we had been talking about making a trip to discover them at the time of his death.

It is late May and the seasons are fighting for control of the weather. Bright, sunny days slapped with cold are followed by howling wet days. We walk around the artist town of Kirdcudbright. We have lunch with Alastair's octogenarian aunt and friendly cousins. We explore the school where Alastair's grandfather was headmaster. We pass the artists' guild, which Alastair's grandfather supported. We throw pebbles into the estuary of the River Dee, where Alastair's father first learned to sail. Alastair grew up with a painting of this very estuary above the fireplace, but he never saw it in the flesh. He never saw it at the close of day, when the russet red of the sky frames the sailing boats spotting the sea. In spirit though I sense that Alastair is there with us. He is in the endless conversations that his mother and I have over pub dinners and bottles of red wine. As I observe the boys chasing each other in a frenzy around Kirdcudbright's ruined castle, I am watching part of Alastair reuniting with his ancestry.

When we pass the house where Alastair's grandfather lived, we discover that it has been turned into a B&B. 'We must stay here, we must,' I insist to his mother.

His mother's eyes shine as she relives her last visit to the house, more than forty years earlier. She was my age then, with her husband carrying the suitcases, while she held her baby daughter in her arms. Life was a calm sea and her smile knew nothing of the losses she would one day bear. We call at the house and ask for a room for the night. The owner of the B&B is aptly called Alastair and he has one room left. I walk up the sweeping, winding stairs blinded by the May light streaming through a giant window before me. Each step, each breath seems to link the past with the present and I am awash with a sense of peace.

Magically tapping into the support of Alastair's ancestors, we awake, his mother, two young sons and I, on the morning of the first anniversary of his death, tucked up warm and cosy in his grandfather's former home.

Alastair shouldn't have died

One month has passed since the first anniversary of Alastair's death. If the time since his death was a baby, it would be walking now. The sharpness of the pain has subsided into a continuous dull ache. Despite my many efforts to keep Alastair close, I have come to accept that the day-to-day life of our family has changed irrevocably and will never go back to how it was. The boys and I are doing ok and life, on the whole, is manageable. I am a survivor of his death.

After too many glasses of wine though, I still cry for Alastair, and for me and for the boys. The painful mantra that burns a hole in the pit of my stomach continues to be: *Alastair should not have died; Alastair should not have died.* My world has calmed down, but it is still a place of quiet chaos, a pit of random indifference. I have fallen out of love with God and I feel He can never make amends.

I sign up for a nine-day spiritual retreat in Germany. I feel so much stronger now than I did when I went to the Buddhist retreat. I am more ready to face myself. The retreat is with Byron Katie, with whom I had done a one-day workshop about ten years earlier. When she was forty-three, Byron Katie woke out of a stupor of depression to a whole new way of seeing life around her. She discovered that the source of her suffering was not what had happened to her in life but what she thought about what happened to her. She found that by questioning her painful thoughts, she became free of them and she stopped suffering. To help others to question their own painful thoughts, she devised a simple worksheet called 'The Work', which I have been using now for ten years on and off. It is made up of four questions and turnarounds.

I have always loved the simplicity, straightforward logic and the ensuing relief of 'The Work'. What I have used most are the turnarounds. If I had a thought like, *Alastair isn't being fair to me*, then I would turn it around to *I am not being fair to me* or *I am not being fair to Alastair*. The turnarounds put me back in the centre of the universe, where I like to be, and give me things to work on within myself, rather than waiting for others to change. It helped dissipate tensions I felt with people around me and allowed me to go back to my usual countenance of friendly optimism. 'The Work' for me was an easy, enjoyable self-help approach.

Only later would I realise how much I had underestimated Katie's work.

I fly to Germany on my own to take part in the retreat and find myself sharing a twin room with a German woman. We exchange niceties and then agree that we will be silent with each other for the duration of the retreat. Over 200 people file into a big conference room to meet with Katie. While many people bustle to get seats near the front, I sit at the back of the room, battling with waves of hope and scepticism that Katie will be able to help me fall in love with life once again.

As an introduction, Katie invites us all to write down the thoughts that are causing us suffering. I dutifully write down in capital letters: 'ALASTAIR SHOULD NOT HAVE DIED.'

'Your painful thoughts are your story,' she tells us gently. 'You are probably very attached to your story and even believe that it is true. I am not asking you to drop it.' She continues, 'I invite you, at this school, to simply investigate who you would be without your story, who you would be if you did not believe that thought.'

I sigh discouraged and go to sleep, awarding scepticism the upper hand.

The next morning, I pair up with a middle-aged woman and we are invited to describe our worst experiences. I recount the well-worn tale of Alastair's death in concise, staccatoed sentences. She listens silently, showing empathy with her eyes and facial gestures. Then it is her turn. She confides to me haltingly that she has a fear of spontaneous combustion; she is afraid that she will suddenly burst into flames. I almost laugh. Even as she talks of the torment this thought has caused her, I dismiss her fear immediately as irrational and ridiculous. '*Her* situation really is a story in her head,' I conclude to myself.

Is it true?

We are in a group session with Katie and one after another, a series of people stand up to speak and cry about their difficult situations. This ranges from a young mixed-race woman who feels that people judge her because of her skin colour to a man who is consumed by his inability to love. As each person stands up, I judge each one and their situations. They are so attached to their stories, which are not even that bad. Nothing irreversible like death has touched them. A fifth person stands up and cries into the microphone about her diabetes. As Katie challenges the truth of her story, she angrily defends how bad her life is. I sigh audibly. Alastair would do anything to be given the option of staying alive through daily insulin shots. I move forward in my back-row chair. It's exciting – I am really getting this. I can see what Katie is talking about. Each one of these people is so blind. It is so obvious that they are clutching on to unquestioned thoughts in their heads. It seems as if they almost *want* to suffer. How they whine needlessly! How they hold on to their stories! I sit back in the chair again, satisfied. It is true, then; I am more perceptive than those around me. I am finally learning something on this retreat. As I relax into the chair, a thought slips casually into my mind, sneaking in from a blind spot backstage. It is more an after-thought than a thought. I nearly miss it: *Not one of these people has a real problem, like I have.*

I sit bolt upright. Oh my God! Hah! Where did that thought come from?

I look up towards the front, where the young woman is still talking about her diabetes. I see myself in her. I *am* her. I am just like everyone else too. I am tightly grasping a narrow, unquestioned thought. My story just seems more real to me than the others' because it is mine. It is me that is blind. It is me that is whining. It is me that wants to suffer. I am so convinced that Alastair should not have died that I have not allowed even the tiniest sliver of space to question it. So, who am I? The knower of all things? The one who knows when everyone should live and die? I glimpse my arrogance and that glimpse is the sliver of space that I need to doubt the veracity of this haunting thought. Is it true that Alastair should not have died? Yes. Can I *absolutely* know that it is true? No.

I sit in this chink of doubt for days. I do not try and convince myself that he should have died or that I am wrong thinking that he shouldn't have died. I merely sit in a state of not-knowing.

Peace. Blessed, blessed peace after fourteen months in a dark, foreboding world.

Unassuming, world-shattering insights come to me in the space of not-knowing. It is not the fact that Alastair died that is making me sad. If I did not love Alastair, then his death would not make me sad. Hey, I could even be relieved to be without him. Then, if it is not his actual death, it is what I believe about his death that is making me sad. Thoughts like: *Death is bad, Alastair misses out on everything when he is dead. Alastair would be better off alive than dead. My life and the boys' lives are worse off without him around, there is no justice, no rhyme or reason to life.* These are all summed up in the thought: *Alastair should not have died.* I cannot absolutely know any of these things. They are not facts, they are ephemeral beliefs or thoughts. Alastair's body died and I cannot change that. It is a fact. I cannot change facts but I can change thoughts. I have often changed my mind and changed beliefs. Heck, I used to believe absolutely that a bearded man in a red suit slipped down my chimney to deliver presents at Christmas. I can weaken the hold thoughts have on me by simply admitting that I do not absolutely know that they are true.

The thought arises time and time again: *Alastair should not have died, Alastair should not have died.* But now I know what to do. Instead of following the thought to the 'poor Alastair', 'poor me', 'horrible world' thoughts and feelings that it leads me towards, I simply hold it in my mind and ask it straight out: 'Is it true?'

Letting go

It is early morning and I am finding it difficult to sleep. I steal out of my hotel room and walk in the gardens, through which runs a fast-moving river. I sit on a wooden bridge over the river, my legs dangling and almost touching the water. In silence, I am twisting Alastair's wedding ring around my finger. Since his death, I have worn his wedding ring on the middle finger of my right hand. His ring is a constant reminder of his love for me. He used to rub his lips along its smooth edge, with a half-smile, when deep in thought or waiting in traffic. I rub the ring along my lips now and feel Alastair's lips against mine.

I slide my own wedding ring off my left hand and look at it. It has a different effect on me. It reminds me of all our broken dreams. At our wedding, my sister read aloud Yeats' poem, 'Aedh wishes for the cloths of heaven'. The final stanza is:

But I, being poor, have only my dreams;
I have spread my dreams under your feet;
Tread softly because you tread on my dreams.

Each time I look at my wedding ring, this poem springs to mind and I wince at the callousness with which my innocence, my youthful naivety and hopefulness were dashed. Existence did not tread softly on my dreams, it stomped up and down on them, breaking them and my heart absolutely. My ring symbolises my victimhood.

As I sit in the stillness of early morning, I let my ring slip silently out of my hand and drop into the water below. With a gentle gurgling, the river swallows its prize and rushes hurriedly on.

Seeds of peace

On the last day of the retreat, we are asked to pair up again and go through a worksheet we had written about our painful thought. I tap the shoulder of an elderly woman in front of me and ask her to be my partner. 'No problem,' she smiles in an American drawl.

We decide to do our work outside in the sun. As we walk out of the room, she tells me that she is, in fact, Irish, but has lived in America for over fifty years and has picked up the accent from there. There is something familiar in the way she speaks and her gentle light-heartedness makes me warm to her. First, she facilitates me doing my worksheet, which is about Alastair's last moments and the thought, *I should have been more present when Alastair was dying.* When we finish, I ask her to read out her painful thought for us to work on.

She looks at her worksheet and then at me. 'Given your situation,' she says, 'we don't have to do it if you are uncomfortable, ok?'

'Why? What is the thought?' I ask.

She looks down at her worksheet and reads: 'I never really lived my life after my husband died.'

'Please,' I smile at her, 'I would love to do 'The Work' with you on that.' It turns out that she was also widowed young. Her husband was murdered randomly in New York. I am taken aback by the similarity of our experiences of losing our husbands so suddenly and the myriad emotions of loneliness, guilt and loss of trust in life that we share. As I facilitate her, she describes to me how, after her husband's death, she moved country with her youngest daughter and undertook several interesting projects. 'But I never allowed myself to truly live after he died. I did lots of things, but they were actions that brought me away from life in truth, rather than towards it,' she tells me. 'In my own heart, I never moved on from his death, I stayed stuck in our story together.'

'If living in different countries and doing interesting projects isn't truly living, then what is living?' I ask her.

'I don't know. I could have written a book or fallen in love again,' she stumbles. 'I don't quite know how to articulate it, but I know how it feels when I am truly alive and when I am not.'

I gape at her. She is a manifestation of a potential future, come back through time to wake me up. Later that day, I fly home to Ireland with seeds of peace planted in my subconscious.

Family dinner

A couple of days after arriving in Ireland after the retreat, my old friend from college L comes to dinner. As usual, I am staying with my parents. My mother is the owner of a magic cooking pot; she always has enough for one more. Well into adulthood, I have often sat at the table between my parents and friends. It has happened naturally as I have no house of my own in Dublin and it has been a way for my parents to know me more fully. At these dinners, my parents are onlookers as I update my friends on my life and respond to what is going on in their worlds. This goes beyond the usual censored, parent-friendly version of events that I share with them when we are on our own.

'Well, I learned more about your antics at that dinner than

in talking to you for the past month,' is a usual post-dinner comment from my father.

L asks me what I got out of the retreat, while my mother serves us stew and my father pours everyone a glass of wine. I breathe deeply, as an answer surfaces. The answer is as much for me as for her. 'You know what?' I begin. 'It helped me to realise that I have been the cause of my suffering since Alastair's death,' I answer with uncharacteristic conciseness.

My mother, breaking from her onlooker protocol, drops the serving spoon, which clatters noisily on the table. 'But you didn't cause his death, Bébhinn,' she says aghast, as she sits down.

I pick up the serving spoon and place it in the bowl of stew. 'No, Mum, I didn't,' I respond calmly, 'but every second of suffering was because of something I believed about his death.'

'What do you mean?' L asks, taking a sip of wine.

'Well, like thinking that death is bad. Can we know that death is something bad and not something beautiful?' I grapple for more examples. 'Or I suffered because of the thought that the boys and I are now alone, or that we cannot be totally happy again. There are so many thoughts that led me to suffer.'

I have to look away from the sceptical expression on my mother's face, so I pick up the bowl of stew and finish serving everyone. The whole table is in silence, until I sit down again beside L.

'I'm not saying it was bad to suffer,' I continue in a conciliatory voice. 'I'm not saying I shouldn't have suffered or shouldn't continue to suffer. I don't mean that I regret how I responded, but now I simply see that it is in my hands.'

Everyone at the table starts to eat and the silence swells around us, save for the gentle clatter of cutlery. I wonder if it is an idea too big for other people to imagine, without living my life for the past year or going on the retreat. As I begin to eat, a wave of gratitude washes over me that this idea rings true in the core of me.

'Mum,' I sigh deeply in relief, taking her hand in mine, 'this is very good news for me. This is very good news indeed. If I know the way into suffering, then I know the way out.'

Glimpse of peace

I am visiting my close friend C in Ireland. At her home, I meet her grandmother, who has not seen me since Alastair's death and who has herself been a widow for over twenty years. She meets me with choking tears and hugs me desperately. 'Poor thing,' she wails at me. 'I know how it is. I know how you are suffering.'

I hug her back, grateful for the love she is offering me and moved by her despair. However, I notice, with endless relief, that I cannot match her despair. She is handing me the thoughts that I am to be pitied and that I am drowning in an endless vat of suffering, but they do not stick to me anymore. The power of the thoughts that Alastair should not have died, that I am a victim of his death, has miraculously crumbled.

The thoughts hang in the air like sound waves, but I am no longer receptive to their frequency.

Part III
PEARLS

'What they undertook to do
They brought to pass;
All things hang like a drop of dew
Upon a blade of grass.'

William Butler Yeats
'Gratitude to the Unknown Instructors'

Finding direction

Each moment of keeping Alastair close is a delicious reprieve from suffering, but each one is so inexorably and damningly transient. What I need is a longer term plan to keep Alastair close to me, longer term activities to provide a detour from the rawness of a life without him.

Quickly, my mind jumps to Alastair's legacy – the donation he left to charity in his will. Supporting international charity efforts is a passion we shared and it is the one thing for which, even now, I can muster some interest. Alastair was active in supporting many different charities over the years, fundraising as a student, leading a medical charity in Peru for eighteen months and through the non-profit practice at the firm where he worked. For the last five years of his life he had been a trustee of the charity Child Health in Rio de Janeiro.

I had this same passion from an early age. When I was eight, I had a dream. Having heard earlier that day that a small number of rich people had all the wealth in Latin America while the rest were poor I stood, in my dream, on a stage in Latin America and told the rich to give to the poor. Everyone clapped and the rich handed over their wealth to the poor. World saved. Me the saviour. Dream complete.

As a teenager, I had been strongly moved and motivated by accounts of international injustice and abandoned children. I used to fundraise for Trócaire, an Irish international development agency, organising other girls in my school to collect change from passers-by for hours on busy Dublin streets.

There was also a spiritual dimension to this passion. Well into early adulthood, I used to say the following words in my prayers and randomly in moments of indecision and uncertainty: 'Lord, make me a handmaiden of your work.' These words comforted me and I repeated them often to provide a sense of purpose in moments of despair.

After university, I had gone straight to volunteer at an orthopaedic clinic in Peru. Since then, I had worked on pro-bono projects for international development charities at the firm where I met Alastair, completed an MSc in Social Policy and had worked with child-focused charities. These real-life experiences had helped me to reduce somewhat my ego-driven mania about saving the world and had lowered my ambitions significantly, but my passion had continued unabated. Alastair and I had first met while working together on a pro-bono project for an international charity. By following our mutual passion, we had found each other.

We had spent our first romantic weekend together in

Buenos Aires. One night we had sat drinking wine under the stars in a square near La Recoleta cemetery, where Eva Perón's body is buried.

'What is your biggest dream?' he had asked me, one bottle in.

I had savoured the stars and the cobblestones. I had savoured the feeling of completeness at being with him. The answer had arisen clearly and naturally. 'I would love to help children who truly need help.'

He had sighed back at me, bathing my face in love. 'You know,' he had begun, taking my hand in his, 'I have always wanted to set up a charity for children. I have always felt that I have been given so much in life and I have this gut-feel that makes me want to share it.'

This shared dream had been a stronger aphrodisiac to us than the Argentinean red wine, the tango music or the entwined dancers that weaved through the square.

Alastair's donation to charity in his will is the spur I need to make this dream a reality. Instead of giving it to an existing charity, I decide to set up a foundation to receive the donation and to raise more money to enable us to set up a child-focused charity. It dawns on me that this idea gracefully offers me the opportunity to keep Alastair close for years to come and to channel all of my energy away from despair and into making our shared dream a reality.

Two months after the first anniversary of Alastair's death, I invite six of our family and friends to an upmarket bar in London's South Bank area. I order a round of beers from an attentive waiter and prop up a picture of Alastair against the wall. Alastair's sister is there, as is my sister, two of Alastair's closest friends and two of my close friends. Now that Alastair, the centrepiece to our relationships, is missing, I am loathe to lose contact with his web of family and friends that were in the process of becoming mine too. I am adamant to keep this group in regular contact, and a joint project might be just the answer.

It is early evening and the bar is almost empty. Light, ambient music is piped through the bar, drowning out the sounds of London traffic and the tourist boats chugging along the Thames. We all sit in comfortable armchairs with light streaming in from the full-length windows behind us. My voice breaks with emotion and nerves as I speak, welcoming everyone to the inaugural meeting of the Board of the Alastair Ramsay Charitable Trust, ARCH. We clink glasses to mark the moment.

'I would like to propose that we set up a child-focused charity in Latin America,' I begin.

S, who oversees child support projects for a large foundation, begins the barrage of questions. 'What will it do?' she asks.

'It will help families with sick children to improve their housing, their income, their psychological health and their nutrition so that the children have a better chance to survive and to thrive,' I rattle off, as I hand out a five-page document to each of them. 'I suggest we set up a social franchise of the charity Child Health for which Alastair was trustee in Rio de Janeiro.'

'How much will it cost?' asks my sister, who sits next to me.

'I have made an initial estimate of £200,000 to set up the

charity and co-fund it for the first three years. In this time, I estimate we will help around fifty families or 200 people, as well as putting in place an organisation to help hundreds more in future years.'

'Where will the other part of the co-funding come from?' asks L.

'It will be raised locally,' I tell her. 'The percentage raised locally will increase each year so that it has a greater chance of being sustainable after year three. So, in the first year, 15 per cent will be raised locally, and ARCH will pay 85 per cent of the budget. In year two 35 per cent will be raised locally and, in year three, 50 per cent.'

'Ha,' P, Alastair's friend, laughs. 'You can take the girl out of business, but you can't take the business out of the girl.'

I laugh with her and continue emphatically. 'I want us to do this well,' I begin. 'I will commit to spending the next three years overseeing this work on a voluntary basis to ensure that it happens.'

There is a collective take-in of breath.

'Wait a second,' my sister retorts. 'How are you going to sustain yourself and the boys?'

'I've thought it all through,' I tell her matter-of-factly. 'I can live off the rent of our house in London. It should be enough for us to live comfortably in Brazil and come back once or twice a year.'

'And what about the boys?' my sister continues, searching for the right argument. 'How are you going to take care of them and do this work in a place where you know nobody? Who is going to help you?'

'I survived Oxford for a year,' I answer defiantly. 'I'll make friends and find a school for the boys. And listen, there is little option for me. I *have* to go. This is the only thing that excites me in any way about the future. This is the only way I can survive my life without Alastair. It lets me keep him close to me, while also starting a new life. If I continue to have a shadow of our old life, the constant comparisons will swallow me whole.'

My sister sits back in her chair.

'Look,' I tell her, more gently now, 'it's only three years and the kids are at adaptable ages. At the end of the three years, I should be clearer, calmer and maybe then I'll know what to do with the rest of my life.'

A silence engulfs the group.

After a couple of minutes, Alastair's sister breaks the silence, smiling at me as she asks, 'So how much money do we need to raise?'

I smile back at her and click back into efficiency mode. 'Alastair's donation is the starting block, as are the donations from family and friends that came in after his death,' I tell her, 'but we still have to raise about £140,000.'

'Well if your mind is made up,' my sister begins, smiling at me too, 'I have some ideas about fundraising in Ireland. We could do events like balls and fun days for children. This way, as well as raising funds, we can bring family and friends together to celebrate Alastair's life.'

'That's perfect,' I chime in. 'The idea behind ARCH is to give all of our family and friends an opportunity to honour Alastair's memory as well as helping a group of children in Latin America.'

Our family and friends had overwhelmed me with their support and well-wishes since Alastair's death and I was filled with a quiet confidence that they would show the same dedication to raising funds for the charity. It seemed as if we were all cut off mid-sentence with Alastair. One minute we were joking light-heartedly and the next moment he was gone. I could sense that many others shared the visceral frustration that seethed within me at not being able to tell him how much he is loved, what a gift his presence has been in our lives. This foundation would give all of us a way to continue the conversation, a concrete way of demonstrating our love and respect for him.

G cuts in. 'This sounds good, but given that you are proposing the project, you need to let us discuss it without you, ok?' G was Alastair's best man at our wedding and is a corporate lawyer. I smile at him and the correctness of the approach, as I stand up from my chair.

As the group discusses the proposal, I sit at the bar and order another beer. I raise my beer to Alastair. 'Well, Al, our dream is becoming reality. We are setting up our charity together.' As I take a drink, I start to cry. My tears fall like pregnant raindrops on the counter and some are soaked up by the paper beer mat. Our dream is becoming reality but not at all in the way I expected. My heart is pummelled by equal measures of fulfilment and despair.

When I go back to the group, they tell me that the proposal is approved. 'We plan to set up fundraising committees of family and friends in the UK, Ireland and the US,' my sister updates me. 'One question remains, though. Where will it be in South America?'

As she asks the question, a vivid dream from the night before flashes before me.

It was a dream of Alastair. He was his usual jovial self and he was swirling around on a black office chair. 'Come to Brazil,' he said to me, 'that's where I am.'

'But don't people notice that you are dead in Brazil?' I asked.

'Well,' he began, 'sometimes I lean back on the chair and I go inside the back of it, but nobody seems to mind very much.'

With that, he demonstrated how his body went straight into the chair and we both laughed. I awoke with absolute clarity.

I smile at my sister. 'Brazil,' I say, 'the boys and I are going back to Brazil.'

Island of magic

A week later, I am curled up on our red sofa in Oxford with the two boys and we leaf through Alastair's heavy leather-bound photo albums from our time in Brazil. I am trying to get ideas for where we could go to set up the charity.

'Look, that's you,' I say to Tom, pointing to a picture of Alastair with Tom in the sling in the cobbled streets of Paraty, south of Rio de Janeiro.

'Baby,' Liam states as he points at a picture of Tom in a yellow and orange babygro underneath the statue of Christ the Redeemer in Rio de Janeiro.

'Yes,' I say hugging him, 'clever boy. That's Tom when he was a baby.'

Alastair and I lived in Rio de Janeiro for three years, but we had left because we did not want to bring up our children in a city marred by so much violence and inequality. We did not want our children growing up looking over their shoulder.

'Rio de Janeiro is out,' I say to myself decidedly, as I leaf quickly through the rest of the album. I pick up another album and see a smiling Alastair waving away the white smoke at a Candomblé spiritual ceremony in the northeastern city of Salvador. Next, he is waving to me from a hillside, with an exquisite sixteenth-century colonial church in the state of Minas Gerais as his backdrop.

'Spida',' Liam shouts with fright as he points at a tarantula by a tent peg.

'It's just a photo, you munchkin,' I laugh, as I tickle him. I look at the photo and remember the yelp I also gave when I spotted that tarantula by our tent when we went camping on the island of Florianópolis in the South of Brazil.

'Ah,' I say to the boys, remembering, 'the island of magic.'

'Magic ice-cream,' Tom says as he points to a photo of Alastair grinning cheekily with two huge ice-creams in his hands. Behind him, waves swell and crash like possessed horses.

'It's beautiful here,' I had shouted to Alastair as I looked up at the dense Atlantic Forest falling straight down to the sea, 'it's just like Rio de Janeiro.'

'Yep,' Alastair had replied as he licked my ice-cream, 'just like Rio, but without the violence.'

Synchronicity

As I drive to pick Liam up from his crèche the next day, my memories of Florianópolis are replaying in my mind. Z, a young English woman who is Liam's key care-worker at the crèche, meets me at the door and asks if we can have a chat. We discuss Liam's daily tantrums and the effect of Alastair's death on this little boy.

'We are going to leave Oxford very soon,' I confide to her. 'We are going back to live in Brazil in early September.' She brightens up.

'What a coincidence,' she says. 'I am going to live in Brazil soon too. My boyfriend is from there and I am going to live with him.'

'Which part of Brazil?' I ask.

'It's in the south,' she begins. I hear the signs of life rev up around us. 'It's an island called Florianópolis.'

I grin at the obviousness of life's conspiracies.

A couple of days later, I ring Dr V, the founder of Child Health in Brazil, and ask her if there is a social franchise in Florianópolis and, if not, whether or not she thinks it would be a good idea to set one up there. I know her well from my time in Rio de Janeiro and her visits to the UK. She answers my call with characteristic enthusiasm.

'Bébhinn,' she half-gasps, 'do you believe in synchronicity?'

I smile down the phone.

'Three days ago I had a phone call from Dr M, a paediatrician from Florianópolis that I know, saying that she is retiring from her job and now has time to help set up a Child Health charity there. She would be your perfect partner.'

I laugh out loud. Synchronicity, it seems, is leading the way.

Brazil or bust

The day we fly to Brazil arrives. We have spent the end of the summer in Ireland surrounded by family and friends and my parents have offered to drive us to Dublin airport, squeezing all of us and our luggage into one car. I have always felt enormous freedom from my parents to travel and live wherever I wanted. When I was in my twenties, living in London and thinking of moving, I discussed it with my parents. Not once did they suggest I come back to Ireland as Irish parents might stereotypically do. Instead, my mother's face lit up with excitement. 'China,' she suggested eagerly, 'why not go to China? Your father and I have never been there and we can go and visit you.'

I thank their adventurous spirit as much as the size of our endless family for this sense of freedom, which offers me the wings of adventure without compromising the eternal roots of home. This time it is different though. Now I am a widow with a three-year-old and a five-year-old in tow. Sometimes, when the ache of Alastair's death is foremost in my heart, I cannot meet my mother's eyes. It is as if she can see into the depth of my despair and feel the endlessness of its echo. She knows how empty I am as I move to the other side of the world, to a city where I have no friends and no family. When two of my brothers come to say goodbye, my mother and I stand together watching as they swing Tom and Liam over their heads to squeals of boyish laughter.

'Those boys need to be near their uncles,' my mother says to me, her voice cracking as she fights back tears.

I gently hug her and whisper into her hair, 'Mum, we have to go. I know this is the right move.'

She hugs me back and clears her throat. 'Well, as I always say, to thine own self be true,' she says, holding me close. 'And we'll come out and visit you next month to make sure you are all ok.'

Her lack of insistence hints to me that she understands the desperation that is driving me onwards. Maybe she guesses that I will wither up if I live a shadow of my former life.

My friend L meets us at the airport and the boys run into her arms when they see her. She has offered to come with us to Brazil and spend a week with us in Rio de Janeiro. During the fourteen-hour flight, the two boys sit on either side of me, their heads nestled into my lap. L is asleep in a different row, exhausted after playing hours of Snap with Tom. L has been going through a marriage breakdown. Her marriage disintegrated around the time Alastair died. She told me of the separation in the wake of Alastair's death and I was left speechless. How could she choose to lose what was so painfully torn away from me?

'Watching you grieve for Alastair,' she had told me, 'only made me more sure that I was making the right decision. I saw you and Alastair together. I could almost taste the certainty you both felt about being together. I want that too. I want to experience that kind of unquenchable love.'

Death and divorce are two faces of loss, but, unlike divorce, death does not dampen love. That is both its solace and its sting.

As I sit on the plane, I am apprehensive about this preparative trip to Brazil. The three years Alastair and I spent in Rio de Janeiro were such a golden time for us. It was here that we had our first home together and got to know each other's friends and family who had hopped on our never-ending conveyor belt of visitors. It was here that we became family to each other and parents to Tom. I know I will feel his absence even more sharply here.

We land before daybreak in Rio's busy international airport, hassled at each side by people offering taxis and thrusting placards with scribbled names of foreign clients. We find a café and drink strong Brazilian coffee to keep us awake as we travel on to our small hotel. The sound of chattering Portuguese and the sight of Brazilian memorabilia littering the airport fills me with a sense of elation and a perfect mixture of familiarity and novelty.

The next day, we awake refreshed and take a bus from the centre to Leblon, south of the city, and slowly lurch our way past the backdrop of Alastair's and my old life together. We pass Alastair's office that overlooks the boat-speckled Botafogo Bay and follow the winding curves of the coastline that brought me home from my work each day. We drive past the Hippie Fair square in Ipanema where Alastair negotiated with great glee the price of paintings that brought an explosion of colour to our grey London afternoons. There now are the traffic lights where we were threatened by a teenager with a gun, while Alastair calmly ignored him. And to the left, the Indian restaurant where Alastair made fun of my insistent demand for spice ('You know, Al, the Brazilians just don't do spice in Oriental food') before I burned my mouth to shreds and could not eat it at all. Here to the right is the paediatrician's office, where we took Tom for his first post-hospital check-up – Alastair insistent that he carry his baby son, with a look of pride and tenderness on his face.

As we struggle off the bus, dragging the pushchair over the turnstile, I am feeling tired and queasy and I am overwhelmed once again by the fact that my body and my mind are just too small to swallow the size of this loss. As the sky darkens and weeps in a sudden burst of torrential rain, I am the sky, and I cannot make out where the rain stops and where my tears begin.

Bemvinda! Welcome!

We escape the heavy memories and a dengue epidemic in Rio de Janeiro and venture down south to the island of Florianópolis. L goes back to Ireland and the boys and I arrive in Florianópolis with one suitcase of belongings each. Each boy grips the baggage trolley tightly as we move through the airport and, in their other hand, they clutch a favourite teddy bear.

Florianópolis, the island of St Catherine, floats on the Atlantic Ocean off the southern Brazilian coast. There is an ancient, 4,000-kilometre trail, the Peabiru Way, which leads many on mythical or religious journeys from the west of South America towards the area around Florianópolis. Some believe that it was built by the native Tupi-Guarani Indians. Legend has it that the Incas walked along this ancient trail from Peru in search of the god Inti, the god of the rising sun to the east. The Tupi-Guarani themselves created part of this trail as they moved from Paraguay to the Brazilian coast in search of the mythical 'Terra Sem Mal' or 'Land Without Evil', which was said to lie someplace in the east, in the Atlantic. There are even some who believe that Jesus's apostle Thomas came from Europe to the southern coast of Brazil. The Tupi-Guarani Indians told the first colonisers of Somé (interpreted as São Tomé or St Thomas), a white-skinned, bearded, barefoot man in a long white shirt who arrived on the southern Brazilian coast, walking on water. Florianópolis is a special place and many in search of peace of spirit have made their way here before us.

The island has a population of 400,000 in the winter, which doubles in the summertime. It is made up of over a hundred beaches and a commercial centre spanning the midwest of the island and part of the mainland. The island and mainland are connected by two bridges. One is the Hercilio Luz Bridge, which lights up the seascape beautifully each evening. It is the postcard image of Florianópolis. Though it looks good, it is of little practical use, as it has been closed for more than twenty years because of its precarious structure. This bridge captures much of Florianópolis: beautiful to look at but disorganised and precarious in many ways.

In Florianópolis, everything begins to fall into place, like a reassuring exhalation. I rent a car and with eyes slapped awake by anticipation I drive us northwards to the sleepy village of Santo Antônio de Lisboa. We drive up the coast road, with the mainland and its mountains to our left, beyond the sea that twinkles invitingly in the midday sun. To our right, we pass the historic centre of Florianópolis, with its brightly coloured, crumbling old buildings and the smell of the public market of fish and spices. I follow the signs for the north of the island and, after thirty minutes of zooming traffic, we arrive at our seaside B&B.

The B&B looks out on the calm bay and is within ten minutes' walk of the village. The pavements to the village are treacherous, turning this ten-minute walk with two small children into a series of stressful jumps on and off the road. In Florianópolis, building the pavement is the responsibility of each individual homeowner. Each one, therefore, leaves a different amount of space, paves it, or not, using different materials and often builds their house right to the edge of the road, leaving no space for anyone to walk. Leisurely walks or cycles are confined to some seafront promenades developed under duress by the local government. The village has a palpable colonial village feel with a weekly market in a cobblestone square that looks out on a calm, boat-speckled sea. The golden red sunset streaking behind a boat-dappled sea fills my heart and head with a sense of eternity.

I find a small, three-bedroom bungalow to rent in a cluster of colonial-style Portuguese houses overlooking the bay. On the beach in front of the house there is a huge acacia tree, with sprawling branches providing perfect shade from the sun. On Sunday afternoons the local men hang bird cages on its branches. Each cage houses one solitary curió bird with its melancholy song. Beneath the singing birds, they sit down around a low, concrete table to play cards. The birdsong sounds of death and despair to me and I wonder how the men would react if I crossed the road and freed one. Perhaps the bird would die within the hour, so atrophied are its wings and instincts.

But is it not better to soar free in the sky for an hour than to live a lifetime in a cage?

Out to sea, the Hercilio Luz Bridge is lit up before us each evening. The house is painted terracotta orange and bound together with whale oil, the custom among colonists. The house suffers from rising damp from the sea and chronic woodworm, two blights on paradise-living on the island of Florianópolis. Despite this, I rent it right away. I ache to be settled with the boys. It feels as if we have been travelling or moving on and off for a year and a half. Although we have stayed in many houses, we have been homeless since Alastair died. Each time we arrive at a new place, Liam looks at me with his blue eyes wide and beseeches, 'Is this our new home, Mummy?'

The collective relief at moving into a more settled home is palpable among the three of us. I feel all wanderlust fall from my shoulders like a worn-out coat. I vow to keep this house as simple as possible. After giving away and farming out Alastair's and my lifetime of furniture and belongings, I am determined never to become heavy with possessions again. I buy three glasses, three mugs, three chairs, three beds, three bowls; it is an ideal home for the fairytale three bears.

We spend the first month getting organised. It is elating to start out in a new place, with no friends, few contacts, no idea of how things get done. It is also complicated. To do anything, from buying a car to signing up to the local video shop, I need an ID number, a CPF. It takes time to get a CPF, so I have to ask people I have just met to lend me their ID numbers. I never ask the same person twice, not wanting to push my luck or give the impression that I am trying to steal anyone's identity.

I am also busy sorting out our visas. Tom was born in Brazil and has a Brazilian passport. Liam and I have a right to reside in Brazil as part of Tom's family. The Federal Police give me a list as long as my arm of documents that I need before I can apply for the visas.

'How long will this take?' I ask on my first visit.

'Once you have all of your documents in order, the police will make a visit to your home some time in the following sixteen months,' I am informed. 'And to finalise the process, I cannot give you any estimate. You can however live in the country, and leave and re-enter the country, while your application is being processed. You may not, however, work during this time.'

I sigh and smile tightly as I leave, being schooled once more in the slow cogs of Brazilian bureaucracy.

I have invited Dr M, the paediatrician interested in co-founding the charity, to have coffee at our house. She is a short, compact woman, with bobbed, dyed-red hair, dark-rimmed glasses and a huge smile. She is in her fifties and walks quickly, energetically. I hold out my hand to greet her when I open the door.

'Bébhinn?' she asks as she moves towards me.

Before I can answer, she hugs me tightly and welcomes me to Florianópolis in a flourish of high-pitched Portuguese. I laugh at her exuberance.

'I am so happy to meet you,' she gushes, eyes glinting. 'Dr V has told me all about you. I'm so sorry to hear about your husband. What a coincidence that we are both ready to set up the charity at the same time.'

I nod enthusiastically at her and invite her into the front room to sit down.

'Let me tell you about me,' she says, as she takes a seat.

Before I sit down beside her, she is telling me the story of her life. She has been a paediatrician in a public hospital for the past thirty years and is also a homeopathic doctor. She is of Italian descent (that's why she speaks so quickly and so much, she tells me) and she is passionate about the work of Child Health.

In a matter of minutes, I realise that I like her. We can work together, I think to myself, as she moves on to tell me, in her frenzied style, of her three children, her grandchild, her diploma with the international University of Peace and, oh yes, she is starting her MBA.

The great ease with which everything is falling into place once we arrive in Florianópolis is giving me the strong, peaceful sense that coming to live here was the right move to make. My name is difficult to pronounce for Brazilians, but it sounds like the word Bemvinda, which is Portuguese for 'welcome'. People I meet in Florianópolis start to call me Bemvinda. Everywhere I go now, I am greeted with a smiling, 'Welcome.'

It chimes perfectly with how I am feeling.

A school for us all

My next priority is to get the boys settled. Tom is already five and Liam is three, so I need a school and playschool for them, yet I have no reference points in this new city. I go online and search furiously for an hour. I narrow the selection down to three schools and organise visits for the following day. The first school is the one English-language school that I find in Florianópolis. Liam is in the pushchair and Tom is holding the handle when we arrive at ten the following morning at a small colonial building in the centre of town. I ring the doorbell and smile encouragingly at Tom. The door is answered by a young teacher who welcomes us in broken English. She brings us on a tour of the building, mixing English and Portuguese with the other children as she passes. Tom and Liam are put at ease by the English and play happily on the plastic toys in the tiny outdoor play area while she shows me around. The space is small, bright and colourful. The young woman shows me the computer that the children start to use at age two. She points out the numbers of the alphabet boldly printed on the walls.

'When the childs are three years old, mostly of them know letters,' she assures me in understandable but not fluent English.

'Do you have other children here who speak English as a first language?' I ask.

'No, we don't,' she says, 'but we like very much have English-speaking childs to help us speak better.'

I frown internally. Do I really want the boys to have to improve their teachers' English?

I call the boys to go, thank the staff for the visit and leave the bright building with crystal clarity that this is not the right school for the boys.

Our next visit is to another school in the centre of the city. It is a Portuguese-language school that uses the Montessori method, which both Tom and Liam have enjoyed before. Though I do not know the method in any depth, I like the free, child-led approach to learning I have witnessed. We arrive at the large, sprawling building at eleven o'clock and walk in through an automatic door. A uniformed security guard immediately approaches us. I stumble over my Portuguese as I tell him we have an appointment to visit the school.

'You need to go to reception in the next building,' he says tightly and shows us the way back out through the automatic door. We enter the reception and it feels more like a company entrance than that of a school. The boys and I sit on white metal chairs until we are called forward to the counter. I explain once again that we are here for a visit to the school and I am asked to wait. There are no toys for the children and they grow restless. We wait for fifteen minutes until a teacher comes to greet us. I leave the pushchair at reception and carry an apprehensive Liam in my arms, as she leads us back out of the reception, through the automatic door and down a long corridor. The sound of children playing in the paved-over playground grows more and more deafening as we move down the corridor. Liam's grasp around my neck tightens.

'There are one thousand students in the school,' the teacher explains as we arrive at one of the classrooms. 'Some come for the morning sessions, some for the afternoon sessions and we also offer full-day education from seven thirty am until six pm.' The classroom is empty and a broad assortment of educational activities is laid out on trays on the low, open shelves. Tom runs in and starts to play with a jigsaw of the human body. I try to put Liam down to let him play, but his arms are locked shut around my neck in fear.

At the end of the visit, I call a taxi from the busy street outside the school, fold the pushchair into the boot and settle into the back with the two boys. It is past midday now and the sun beats down on us mercilessly through the window of the taxi. Inefficient air conditioning hums noisily from the front of the car. As Liam falls asleep on my lap and Tom looks out the window, I discount the Montessori school as well. How could I leave Liam in that big jungle of a school? Memories of his daily tantrums at his nursery in Oxford fill me with a feeling of despair.

Only one school left now: a Waldorf or Steiner school and I do not feel too confident about it. I chose to visit this school because it uses an educational approach that Alastair's sister had mentioned to me before. She had sent her children to a Waldorf school for a few years in Namibia and had spoken on occasion about its play-based education. I know almost nothing about this educational approach, but had almost dismissed it based on a misplaced belief that it was most suitable for children with learning difficulties, and not the right school for my budding academics. I am visiting the school more out of curiosity than genuine interest for the boys.

By the time we arrive at the school, Tom and I are hot and bothered and Liam is sleeping and sweating in my arms. I struggle out of the car and huff with effort as I unfold the pushchair offered by the taxi driver, while still holding Liam. I drop Liam onto the pushchair in relief. I ring on a small bell and am led through a red wooden gate into the schoolyard. Huddled around the yard are three low buildings that look more like little houses than classrooms. The yard is a mixture of dirt floor, several low trees sprawling their branches like up-side-down octopi about us, and a wooden play area built around the trees. I have stepped back in time to the 1920s. I am led to a classroom, where I meet S, one of the playschool teachers. I leave Liam in the shaded porch and enter the classroom, which also seems to be from a different era, a simpler time. The floor, the table and the chairs are all made of unadorned brown wood. There are no bright colours on the walls, no letters or numbers and no plastic toys. There are several wooden crates piled up on one side of the room, with a big wicker chest of soft balls made of wool. On the other side of the room, a plum-red cloth is hung over a wire and fanned out at the sides by crates to make a small house, which has a table inside made out of the slice of a tree stump. Tom sits down on the floor to play with a wooden marble labyrinth and is quickly absorbed. S, a woman of German descent in her mid-forties, invites me to sit down next to her on one of the tiny children's chairs that are laid out in a circle in the centre of the room. I sit down in front of a low table, which is covered in feathers, leaves and shells. Behind the table is a swirling watercolour of the Virgin Mary with the baby Jesus in her arms.

How different this is to the bright colours and overwhelming visual stimulation of the two other schools I visited. How homely it is compared to the business and academic focus of most children's playschools I have known.

As I sit in the child's chair, I have the profound sense that I have come home.

As S and I converse, the story of Alastair's death and the Child Health project pours out of me. I am hot and tired from dragging the boys around all morning and I burst into tears before her. She listens to me patiently and then hugs me gently. As I calm down, she tells me briefly that Waldorf schools were inspired by the educational teachings of Rudolf Steiner, an Austrian who was born in the second half of the nineteenth century, who was a remarkable philosopher, spiritual scientist and prolific author.

When I ask her what the educational approach is, she smiles at me and pats my hand. 'This is a place for your children to develop all aspects of themselves, including the spiritual,' she tells me. 'But be warned,' she laughs at me, 'this school is for the whole family, not just the children.'

The school promises to be the ideal nest to embrace my two *gringo* boys as they learn a new language and culture. I nearly leap with joy when she tells me that the boys will be together in her classroom, which caters for children from ages three to six. 'Oh, and don't worry about the language barrier,' she smiles at me. 'I used to live in England and speak English fluently.'

I sign both boys up to the school and they can start right away. On their first day, Tom bounds in on arrival, undeterred by the unfamiliar surroundings and new language, and clasps hands with a boy in his class. Liam hovers behind my legs, peeping out occasionally to watch his brother closely. What a gift for Liam and for me that Tom will be right next to him to ease him into this new life.

In the afternoons, I organise the boys' first swimming lessons and football classes. Within a couple of weeks, our daily routine resembles that of any family with small children in Oxford or Dublin. Middle-class childhoods, I realise, are a global phenomenon.

Late emigrants

The weather is not what we expected. I was looking forward to Rio de Janeiro weather and its searing, year-long, seasonless heat. I left all warm clothes in Ireland, thinking smugly that I would not need them again for quite a while. I am quick to discover first hand that Brazil is made up of many different countries within one nation, each with its own climate and cultural mix. In the south of Brazil, September heralds wet and cold days and the houses are ill-equipped to deal with the climate. It is a wet cold, making it hard to dry clothes or to get warm indoors, where central heating is a foreign concept. I feel my shoulders tense each time I enter the house and I struggle to get warm in bed, despite my heavy woollen blankets. For a month after we arrive it rains solidly, causing mudslides on the roadsides and endless traffic jams.

My parents come to visit us at the end of September. 'Congratulations on having found the only place on earth that sees more rain than Ireland,' my father says, laughingly patting me on the back.

At school, the other children wear wellies and scarves, while all I have for the boys are sandals and shorts. Their teacher tut-tuts me into re-buying them an Irish wardrobe. The other children, running around in their woollen, hand-knitted jumpers look on the whole like any group of Irish or English children. In sharp contrast to Rio de Janeiro and the typical foreigners' view of Brazilians' dark skin colour, most children in Florianópolis are fair-skinned and fair-haired, many blonde and some blue-eyed children laughing as they skip rope or climb exotic fruit trees. The south of Brazil was colonised by a mixture of Germans, Italians and Portuguese, and their ancestry is clear to see at every turn. In some cities inland from Florianópolis, remnants of German and Italian can still be heard, architecture mirrors century-old European styles and polenta, pasta, German cakes and decorated biscuits fill the shops' shelves. Germany's Oktoberfest is a high-profile annual celebration here, replete with beer, lederhosen and knee-clapping. The fact that my two blond-haired, milk-white sons do not stand out in the crowd or in the school photo is a relief to me. They would have been the two obvious *gringos* in Rio de Janeiro, but here, as their Portuguese improves and their accents become that of the local *manézinho*, they can easily blend in with all the other European emigrants.

They are just a century or two late.

No broken family

To my great relief, I find that there is nothing strange about being a single woman in Brazil starting a new life on my own with two small boys. I am like many other women my age here, where the family structures are much more fluid than in England and certainly more so than in Ireland. I discover that in Florianópolis, living together, living together apart, separation, divorce, remarrying and composite families are all much more prevalent and accepted. I soon collect friends who are single with small children, divorced and sharing custody of their children, childless and in their forties (and happy about it), or have children with two or three different fathers. The fluidity of family structures is a great relief to me. There is no stigma towards me or towards my two fatherless boys. In the boys' class contact list that does the rounds at each group parent–teacher meeting, I note that several children have no contact details for their father. Alastair's name, with no email address or mobile phone number below it, does not scream out our family's brokenness. Our family, by Brazilian terms, is not broken. It is just one of the endless combinations of family that Brazil shelters.

The boys and I adopt an abandoned, mostly Labrador puppy and call him Scruffy Al, to have an Al in the house once again. Scruffy Al is a black Labrador, just the dog that Alastair always wanted to have. Another one of Alastair's dreams ticked off, I think to myself as I stroke the mischievous pup. I cannot bring myself to adopt just one dog. What if he is lonely? I cannot bear my own feelings mirrored in any other living being, so I adopt Scruffy Al's sister as well. We call her Samba, which is the name Alastair and I had chosen for the dog we had planned to adopt when the boys were a bit bigger. The dogs quickly become a part of our everyday, their presence helping me to feel safer and sleep better at night. They give me more jobs to do too, more energy to direct towards others: just what I need for now.

I am finding that Florianópolis is a wonderful, welcoming place to raise children on my own. There are no strict English seven o'clock bedtimes. In the restaurants in the evenings, people play with the boys, giving them the thumbs-up or high-fives and greeting them as *alemães* (Germans/foreigners) in friendly voices. We are far from the disapproving gazes in England and Ireland, where restaurants in the evenings are not the right place for small children. I think back to Oxford, where I had finally ventured out to a riverside restaurant with the boys to break up a long, lonely evening. Just as we were enjoying watching the peacock and the ducks on the river and the two boys were excitedly pointing out all the things they could spot, an elderly man came up to me and asked me, in disapproving tones, to keep my children quiet. I remember my sense of shock and the welling tears in my eyes as I turned to the boys, self-conscious now and uncomfortable on our first evening out.

As some of these initial evenings stretch before me in Florianópolis in unending loneliness, I can take the boys out to a local restaurant and savour the comfort and bustling noise of casual, friendly company.

The genie's lamp

At the end of September, the boys are at school and I am exploring the centre of Florianópolis. I am walking down a cobblestone street when I come across a bookshop. I stand outside, with my hand resting on the handle of the door. 'The book I find here,' I say to myself, 'will guide me.'

I have done this once before, when I was in my early twenties in Peru. In a tiny bookshop in the middle of the Peruvian Amazon, I found a Spanish translation of Erich Fromm's *The Art of Loving*. It guided me towards an embryonic understanding of mature love. The book was the first gift I gave to Alastair. On the first page, I wrote:

Dear Alastair,
If love is an art, may you master it.
If it is a gift, may you be blessed with it.
If you will live it, let me share it with you.

I press down on the door handle of the bookshop and hear the tinkle of the bell as I enter. I move slowly around the empty shop, waiting for the book to leap out at me. Rows and rows of books stand before me. Doubt is completely absent. I know I will find what I need to find. Suddenly, it is before me. I stop and smile with all of myself. A bright, colourful book is on display for me. 'So it's you who will guide me,' I laugh to myself as I take the book in my hand. It is like meeting someone from your distant childhood and realising you are in love with him. It is both a gentle surprise and recognition of something you already knew.

The book is a jazzed-up reprint of *Learning to Silence the Mind*, by the Indian mystic Osho. I buy it and go to a nearby café where I fall heart-first into the book. I read of Osho's dynamic meditations, which seem to fit with me and my frenetic mind. The memory of the fleeting glimpses of peace that meditation gave me on the Buddhist retreat returns again and again. The whisper of deep-rooted change that counselling pointed out to me ushers me on. The journey into myself sits in the wings, calling my name softly and patiently.

I pay for my coffee and hurry to my first homeopathic appointment with Dr M. Her office is in a high commercial building, one block from the boardwalk. Outside her window, several tall apartment buildings with darkened windows block us in, but if you strain your neck you can get a glimpse of the sea.

'Tell me everything,' she invites with a gesture of her hand.

I unload my story on her. She writes furiously in illegible scrawl on an A4 sheet of paper, prodding me for clarification from time to time. My Portuguese trips me up occasionally, but the weeks of having no one to speak to and the tension of a new beginning unleashes the story of Alastair's death and of the subsequent fifteen months like a raging torrent. I sit back in my chair exhausted as she makes her final scribbles on the page. Several minutes pass and I relax into the chair.

She finishes writing and turns her attention once again to me. From her desk, she picks up a small genie's lamp. 'Now,' she says as she hands the genie's lamp to me, 'make your wish.'

My heart is still beating fast from the adrenaline of my outpouring. The stockpile of exhaustion accumulated during Alastair's death and the last fifteen months rises within me and my mind empties itself into a silent clarity. My wish is printed in capital letters in my mind's eye and I see grainy images of family life once again. I sigh as I voice it: 'I WANT MY HUSBAND BACK.'

Yogic opportunities

At the beginning of October, a month after my arrival in Brazil, I sign up for a yoga class in the local church hall. On a Thursday evening, I welcome the babysitter, before jumping in the car alone to go to my first class. I do yoga asanas under the naked wooden rafters of the church hall, which is lit up by the magical rust-coloured sunset over the Santo Antônio de Lisboa inlet. I sigh in contentment. The teacher, W, is an attractive man of Italian descent in his forties, and he welcomes me with endearingly accented English. As I sign up to the class afterwards, he shoots questions at me.

'Are you here alone? Husband, boyfriend?'

I laugh at his directness and tell him I am here with two young men, aged three and five.

W provides low-cost yoga classes to the community. For years, he has been teaching yoga to a large following of women over seventy in the afternoons and a younger group in the evenings. Most people pay the small monthly fee he asks. Those who can pay more do so, and those that cannot pay give him fruit from their gardens or bake him cakes.

It is dark outside when I leave the yoga class. I nip into the local shop to buy milk for the boys' breakfast and then jump into the car to go home. As I drive, I see W on the road and offer him a lift.

'You know you've got no lights on,' W laughs at me as he sits into the car beside me.

'God,' I yelp and turn on the lights that stream out onto the road before us. 'I think you've just saved my life,' I laugh at him. There is a light-hearted frisson of attraction and I smile to myself in the darkness of the car.

Brazilian charm

Two days later, my phone rings as I am walking down a busy road. It is W and I smile as I recognise his voice. It is hard to hear him over the traffic. I put my hand over one ear, scrunch up my face and nestle the phone against my other ear to hear him.

'Now that I saved your life in the car, I was wondering if you could save mine,' he began. 'It's my birthday this week and all of my friends are away. Would you like to have dinner with me?' Before I could answer, he adds, 'And bring your children along. I would love to meet them.'

I nearly laugh down the phone. 'Brazilians are gooood,' I admit quietly to myself, as I admire his approach. 'We'd love to,' I shout down the phone above the sound of roaring traffic. As I hang up, I take three skips down the road. A wide grin spreads across my face. For the first time in a long time, I feel young and attractive again.

First date

On the night of our date with W, I sit the boys down in our small, wooden-floored sitting room with their backs to the sea outside, to watch a cartoon DVD while I get dressed.

'What should I wear?' I tut to myself as I look through my small collection of clothes. I feel like a teenager again and scold myself for being so nervous. 'Jesus, Bébhinn, you're thirty-two, it's not like you haven't been on a date before.' I rifle through the few outfits I have and choose a colourful wrap-around dress. I try it on and hold up looped earrings to my ears. *Very Brazilian*, I think as I preen before the mirror, *and even a bit fun.*

As I look in the mirror, I search my eyes and my heart for feelings of guilt for going on a date with a man other than Alastair. To my relief, there is not a shadow of guilt there. Alastair and W have nothing to do with each other. This is a completely different story. 'I guess I'm ready,' I sigh and smile at myself encouragingly in the mirror. To beat the butterflies in my stomach, I bustle the boys into action and bundle them into the car to go on our first family date. We go to a charming local courtyard restaurant, with a tree for the boys to climb and paper and pencils for them to draw on. Somehow, W and

I manage to have an easy, fun conversation, punctuated by the boys' endless demands and questions. I smile as he tells me that he has been a passionate follower of Osho, my newly confirmed mystic guide, for over twenty years.

The boys take to W with no great ceremony – a new friend to lift them on his shoulders. By the end of the evening, I have a strong desire to run my hand against the back of his neck as I pass his chair. Instead, I whoosh Liam into my arms and sit down to draw with him, smiling quietly to myself at the possibility that is opening up before me.

Starting to work

Once we are settled, I set about understanding poverty in Florianópolis and the demand for the charity that we plan to set up. While the boys are at school, I do some research. I find that there are an estimated 60,000 people living in poor conditions on the island, three times as many as there had been twenty years ago. An estimated 15 per cent of the island's population lives in slum-like areas characterised by precarious wooden huts and limited sanitation and other public services. I read this report twice before it sinks in. It is hard to imagine so many people in poverty when you sit on one of the many idyllic beaches on the island or go out to dinner in the lively Lagoa area. Poverty is hidden away here, swept out of sight of the tourists.

In mid-October, Dr M and I meet for a strong espresso in the neon-plastic food court of a small shopping centre near the hospital. 'We need to present the idea to the Children's Hospital,' Dr M enthuses. 'That will give us a better idea of whether or not there really is demand for the Child Health Programme.'

'Do you know anyone at the Children's Hospital?' I ask as I take a tentative sip of tar-strength coffee.

'Oh yes,' Dr M laughs. 'I know the director very well, we were interns together. I'll give him a call right now.'

I settle into my chair as Dr M takes out her mobile phone and rings the director. I am learning that this is how she works. She is incredibly well-connected and action-oriented.

'Next Thursday at ten a.m.,' she smiles as she puts down the phone.

World unfolding as it should

Dr M and I meet outside the hospital that Thursday just before ten o'clock. The hospital is a large, sprawling grey building that does not look unlike a hospital in Dublin. Its breath stinks of suffering and disinfectant. It is the one child-only hospital in the state and I have read from its website that it has 138 active beds and hospitalises over 8,000 children a year. Most of the children come from Florianópolis or nearby municipalities, with about a third coming from the far-off interior of the state.

We receive our visitors' badges and walk together to the director's office. Dr M waves to several people as we walk down the sanitised corridors. The director of the hospital welcomes us with a large smile. Like Dr M, he is in his mid-fifties. He wears dark-rimmed glasses and is wearing a suit rather than the white coat I had expected. With a surprising mix of good nature and efficiency, he sits us down on a couch in his office and invites us to present the idea of Child Health to him. He listens intently and responds in factual, staccato statements. 'This isn't Rio de Janeiro with its endless *favelas* (shanty towns), but we do have need for this programme in Florianópolis,' he tells us. 'There are families here who need a wide array of supports to provide a healthy environment for their children. There is growing poverty in the peripheral cities of Florianópolis, such as São José, where many families are attracted to the tourist and commercial centre of Florianópolis. Many end up living in dire situations, vulnerable to illness, floods, violence and drug-trafficking. Many of their children wind up here.'

He invites me to meet with representatives of other sectors of the Children's Hospital, such as the HIV/AIDS clinic and social services, and asks his secretary to write out names and phone numbers. With that, he smiles at us, stands up, shakes our hands and leads us to the door. Over the next month, I meet with the different representatives he has suggested. In the HIV/AIDS clinic, the nurse describes how a family with a HIV-positive child receiving ARVs, or antiretroviral drugs, simply does not have a fridge to keep the medicines. The social workers describe more complex problems, such as a local single mother with psychiatric problems and three children, one of whom has a chronic illness. This child is regularly hospitalised because of the mother's struggle to manage his illness while also taking care of herself, her other two children and the daily challenges of living in one of the poorest and most isolated areas of the island of Florianópolis.

As my research and meetings confirm the need for the charity, I continue to grapple with the appropriateness of what I am doing. Why am I, an Irish woman, representing an Englishman and our mostly Northern-hemisphere friends, families and colleagues, leading an effort to set up a charity in the south of Brazil? What convoluted psychological issues are driving me to want to meddle in other people's lives anyway?

My mind justifies quickly. Both Alastair and I saw despairing poverty on our travels and felt a strong gratitude for our own comfortable lives. This moved Alastair and moves me still.

My mind whirrs on. Should I instead stay at home and concentrate on the social needs in Ireland, or even England, if I want to contribute? Again, my mind jumps to justification. This work is really Brazilian, as it is replicating a Brazilian home-grown support service that has demonstrated its effectiveness. The world is global and we are global citizens with global responsibilities, so why not contribute in Brazil? Facts and figures demonstrate that Brazil has more demand and less relative supply of effective poverty-alleviation policies or programmes than Ireland or England, so we can make a bigger difference here. Both Alastair and I had always been mesmerised by the adventure associated with going to exotic places to do humanitarian work, a tragic-romantic image that moved us in a way that a drab estate in London or Dublin just failed to do. I recognise too that at its core, this move allows me to maintain a day-to-day relationship with Alastair, while also distancing myself from living a shadow of my former life in England or Ireland.

While thinking through this jumble of reasons and justifications, I experience a sense of quiet. In this silence, blasted into being since Alastair's sudden death, what arises is a desire to honour Alastair, to keep him close to me, and to give of myself. I have the sense that this impulse is bigger than my grasping mind can comprehend. It is clear to me that I am exactly where I should be in the universe and the world truly is unfolding as it should.

Child Health Florianópolis: Alastair's daughter

It is a breathtakingly beautiful day, and the front of our little house is full of sun and the sounds of the sea and the season's first trickle of tourists. It is early December 2008, more than a year and a half after Alastair's death and days after what would have been his forty-first birthday. We have been in Florianópolis for just over three months. In dribs and drabs, a group of fifteen new friends arrive at the house and sit down to drink a cold beer together. They are here to witness the birth, the baptism and the celebration of the organisation, Child Health Florianópolis.

The core of the group is the initial board of Child Health Florianópolis. When I arrived in Florianópolis, I had no idea how I would pull together a group of local people whom I could trust and who would trust me back to set up the organisation. With the ARCH Foundation, I could recruit friends and family for the board, but here I had few connections. On arrival, I had only two contacts: Dr M and Z, Liam's nursery teacher in Oxford, who has now moved to live here with her boyfriend. These two contacts proved enough, however, to reveal the perfect founding board for Child Health Florianópolis.

The board of directors, made up of a vice-chairperson and chairperson, has the ultimate responsibility and Dr M and I respectively take on these positions. 'You are the mother and

I am the godmother of the organisation,' Dr M emphasises as she encourages me to be the organisation's first chairperson.

Apart from the board of directors, we need three people to compose the fiscal board in order to legally set up Child Health Florianópolis. Dr M has introduced me to T, the future president of a local Rotary Club and a successful business woman and entrepreneur. She visited Child Health in Rio de Janeiro before agreeing to join us.

I met Z and her boyfriend for dinner at a restaurant by the sea and discovered to my delight that he is the director of the first Community Institute in Florianópolis, which bridges international and national resources with local charities. He is a perfect candidate for the board. On invitation, he accepted. He, in turn, recommended M, Child Health Florianopólis' first employee who had started work a month earlier helping to develop a social business plan. She is a young, competent dynamo who mixes perfectly her visible German ancestry with a passion for samba. M, in turn, introduced me to A. I greet A as he arrives at the house. He is a tall, thin man and is wearing glasses and a friendly smile. He is an accountant and an entrepreneur, which is an unusual mix in any country. He is quietly enthusiastic about the charity and has committed free accounting support from his organisation. Something about his presence reassures me. As I kiss his cheek in greeting, I realise that he reminds me in several ways of Alastair and this helps to still my nerves.

The rest of the group is made up of new friends who have generously and happily welcomed the boys and me to Brazil. We are a random mix of Brazilians, English and Irish, relaxing and chatting, while being entertained by, and entertaining, the boys. W is there, having become a regular fixture in our lives after our first date.

'Welcome to the birth of Child Health Florianópolis,' I greet everyone. 'Thank you all for coming and for supporting this initiative. This is a dream that I shared with my husband, Alastair, and now I can share with each one of you.'

Everyone claps and raises their glasses.

'I would like to thank W, who helped me get the house ready today to receive you all,' I say smiling at W, who is leaning against the frame of the door. 'I have what everyone wants,' I continue lightheartedly, 'a devoted husband and a helpful boyfriend.' Everyone laughs with me. 'Now M, Child Health Florianópolis' first employee, will talk us through the organisation's Memorandum and Articles and then we will have a vote to approve it.' I cede the floor to M and stand by W in the doorway. He puts his arm over my shoulder and hugs me to him.

The vote is unanimous and then I stand before the group once again. 'Now that Child Health Florianópolis has been born, we will move on to baptise it. If everyone can take a daisy from the large flower pot outside and join me across the road on the beach.'

There is a magic energy of joy and celebration in the air, as the group crosses the road and kicks off their shoes on the sand. I crack open some sparkling wine and fill our plastic champagne glasses, with the sand hungrily soaking up the overspill. 'To Child Health Florianópolis,' I say, as we all raise our glasses.

When the sparkling wine is finished, each of us wades into

the sea and throws our flower out to Iemanjá, the goddess of the sea, and makes our wishes for the organisation.

'Healthy children,' one friend shouts as she throws her daisy as far as she can.

'Dignity,' another calls out.

Wishes for 'work of love', 'happiness', 'impact' are sung out above the sound of the endless ebb and flow of the wavelets. I stand laughing with the group and a memory surfaces. Six years earlier, Alastair and I stood on a different Brazilian beach, surrounded by our friends in Rio de Janeiro and threw flowers into the sea, making our wishes for the future before we headed back to Ireland to get married. Somehow, in the joy of this Santo Antônio moment, it seems like a continuation and a new beginning, as each wave flowing over my feet is new and yet the sea is eternally unchanging.

As we move back across the road to celebrate with a typical meal of fried fish, rice, chips and beans in our next-door restaurant, I am filled with a great sense of gratitude and completeness. I think of Alastair and his burning desire to have a daughter and smile at the thought that 'organisation' in Portuguese is a feminine word.

As I take one last look at the sea speckled with daisies, I offer this up to Alastair. 'This, my love, is the daughter that you wanted, created by the two of us, supported by all our friends and family.'

Teenage ideals

It is two months later, in early February 2009, when we gather for the official launch of Child Health Florianópolis. I am together with fifty other people in a large open room with big windows looking out at the sea. The sun catches the water in its wink and there is a sparkle to the room as the launch begins. We all sit in a circle. There is a small group of staff, volunteers and board members in official T-shirts. A couple of journalists sit with pen and paper to hand. The room is backstage at a big music venue. After the launch, a benefit show will be held for the charity. The musician, D, is well known in Ireland and a childhood friend of mine. He has organised a mini-tour in Latin America around doing a benefit launch show for Child Health Florianópolis. He has also invited SJ, a well-known Brazilian musician and social activist, to sing with him.

D's visit creates a whirlwind of emotions for me. As idealistic teenagers in Dublin in the 1990s, he and I were involved in raising money for international charities. Each year from the age of seventeen, he and his band would play music on O'Connell Street along with other bands for a week of fundraising. I would be nearby, singing quietly to their music, in my bottle-green uniform with my badly ironed kilt, a charity sash across my chest and a fundraising bucket in my hands. Here we are again, fifteen years later, doing the same thing.

The heart of the launch is in the stories told by two mothers, C and G, who we invited from Rio de Janeiro. They have gone through the Child Health Programme there. C stands before the group and begins to cry. One of the volunteers touches her arm gently and she composes herself.

'My child was extremely ill when he was born,' she begins. 'He was my first child and I was already forty years old. Who would care about a forty-year-old mother, alone with a sick child? When he was sick, everything started to fall apart. I couldn't work, I couldn't pay any bills. I had nowhere to turn.' Her voice gets stronger now, as all around her listen intently. 'I was invited to the Child Health Programme and, to tell you the truth, I was wary of these strangers who wanted to help me. I started with one foot behind, ready to leave at any moment.' C was living her story now as she spoke, and we were all living it through her. 'Child Health gave me help, all kinds of help, including medicines, improvements to my home and the chance to take some training courses. Most of all they helped me to free myself from the desperation I was feeling and truly believe that I could do it. Now,' she continues, looking around the room with her head high, 'my son's health is stable, I have a good income and I have hope in my life.'

There is a moment of silence as she finishes and I look about the room at the tear-streaked faces mirroring my own. Then the room erupts in applause.

During D's show, he invites C and me on stage to say a few words about the charity to an audience of approximately 1,000 people. 'What a way to start off this project,' I say to the crowd. 'I invite everyone to join our work by giving a donation or as a volunteer. Let's make helping others creative and fun.'

D hugs me on the stage when we finish and I marvel at the beauty of two teenage friends maintaining their ideals and their friendship. I feel an extraordinary rush of love for my dimpled soul-friend. 'What crazy, wonderful world is this?' I ask him, blinded by the spotlights.

D begins to sing. 'And so it is, just like you said it would be, life goes easy on me, most of the time.'

Family fortunes

Our first family joins the programme in March – a mother who arrives with her two little boys, who remind me of younger versions of Tom and Liam. P, the older of the two, has strong wilful brown eyes like Tom and he sits without hesitation between my knees and builds a tower of green and blue tubes, delightedly turning the cogged wheel to watch the tower twirl. His brother, E, is more reluctant, but as the morning wears on, he climbs into my arms, soother in mouth, and wills me to walk him around the one room of Friendship House. In the far corner of the room, the boys' mother, L, looks wafer-thin in a plastic white chair. Her cheeks are sunken and her body covered in pock marks.

Hours earlier, at a quarter to six in the morning, she had woken her two little boys, dressed them in their best clothes and dragged them to the bus-stop – a sleepy and truculent two-year-old and his one-year-old baby brother. Here she started the two-hour journey to cross the picture-postcard bridge of Florianópolis to get to the Children's Hospital. This is a journey she knows too well.

It is a journey she has travelled repeatedly in the two short years of P and E's lives. She tells me offhand that she has only one more appointment for E, but that P will be back every three months from now on. And then she goes quiet. E is lucky; P less so. P laughs as he hands me another piece of the Thomas the Tank Engine jigsaw, unaware that he is HIV-positive.

As L talks to the social worker, she tells her of her other three children, one of whom at fourteen has disappeared. She does not want to involve the police, because she might get him into trouble. The family lives in a damp basement in a poor area on the periphery of Florianópolis, where mother and father are both HIV-positive and have pneumonia. The father works in construction, but work is sporadic and the pneumonia has left him weak. He has a hard time accepting his HIV-positive status. L seems hardened and distrustful and she asks forcefully for charity. She demands a new house, a mattress, more food. At the end of the session, she rushes outside, lights up a cigarette and lets out a sigh.

Six months later, I stumble across the first tentative impact on this family's life and I am overcome by elation and humility. During one of the handicraft workshops that we offer to the mothers, L and I sit opposite each other, both embroidering T-shirts with patchwork outlines of the little girl on the Child Health logo. I am trying to thread my needle, as L deftly threads hers and sets to work. L holds up her T-shirt for the handicraft instructor to have a look and beams as her good work is praised. Though just thirty-seven, her smile shows her one and only top-level tooth, rotten black, at the front of her mouth. I smile with her as I try to keep up with her embroidering, and she begins to talk.

'You know,' she says, 'I have no reason to be unhappy now.'

Her words stop me in my tracks and I put down my needle to listen. She rethreads a needle and continues. 'We moved house last week,' she continues. 'We are on the same road, but it is a good house, with a little yard for the boys to play outside and it is right next to the shop. I have a neighbour and we've already started helping each other with the kids. I made my husband move from the basement, which belonged to his sister, because my bronchitis was not going away because of that damp. I paid for the mover's van with the money I made from the handicraft I make here. The rent is R$250 a month,' she continues, 'but my husband just got a new job, delivering bricks for construction. He is making R$700 a month and he is on the books, so if he gets sick again, he won't lose his job.'

'That's great,' I smile.

'Yes, and with the money I am getting from making handicraft I can pay for the things my sons need. What I need now is to get P into a crèche, so that he can mix with other kids and I can do more work.'

I feel an overwhelming desire to whoop for joy, but I pull my attention back to my embroidering and try to catch up. Over a hot, black coffee, L tells me she has been to the doctor with P and that his viral count is better than before. She says that she is now taking her medication without fail, though her husband will not treat himself. 'I was talking to M last month,' she says. M is another mother who has AIDS and has two daughters with HIV. 'M was saying that sometimes she feels like giving up and killing herself, but I told her that we have to look after ourselves or who will mind our children?'

We sit back to our embroidery and a new mother joins us. She is schizophrenic and is a single mother of three children, each of whom has health issues. Her eldest son, who is thirteen, is slowly going blind. She talks nervously, impulsively. She turns to L and asks what illness her son has. With a slight hesitation, but a defiant voice, L tells her that P is HIV-positive. This silences the woman's nervous chatter. 'I am not ashamed of saying it,' says L with a spark of vulnerability. 'Look at my son, he is a healthy boy and I am doing a good job taking care of him.'

'You're right not to be ashamed,' I say to L, admiring her courage. 'In a way, we all have HIV, none of us knows when we are going to die.'

We continue to embroider the T-shirts and, within me, my admiration for L grows. The transformation of her life circumstances in these six months is startling. And at the heart of this incredible change is a growing self-esteem. She has embraced the handicraft programme wholeheartedly and quickly turned her hand to anything that the instructor introduced to her. We gave her a sewing machine and she is starting to make crafts at home. Her dream is to have a little shop and she has started selling her creations in the programme's weekly market stall. She is no longer asking for charity, but is running after opportunities.

I cradle this information and, amidst the sense of elation, a question comes to mind: To what extent is this transformation due to the programme? The programme has given food, hygiene products, medicine, nappies, clothes, a mattress and blankets to the family. L has also received nutritional benefits and dental advice. We have provided an opportunity to produce and sell handicraft products and have helped her regulate her working papers. We have ensured that the children are vaccinated, attending school and that her son is attending doctors' appointments. We have encouraged her to treat herself too, providing bus fares to the hospital, and we have provided group and individual counselling support over these six months.

But the transformation has come from her.

'Do you think the programme helped your life to get better?' I ask her.

This time it is she who puts down her needle. 'This project is really important to me,' she says. 'The people treat me differently here. I feel more comfortable here than I feel with my own in-laws or my own mother. I don't like doing the art therapy much, but I love the handicraft. I know all of you can help me, but I know that I have to help myself too.'

Her words caress me in a way I have never experienced before and I am overwhelmed by a sense of humility. As I drive to pick Tom and Liam up from school that lunch-time, I watch as a sense of admiration, grace and gratitude take centre stage within me.

Giving and receiving

Over these first six months, Child Health Florianópolis becomes a meeting place of two distinct cultures. On the one hand, we have a group of volunteers (psychologists, educators, dentist, architect) and a small, modestly paid staff (social worker, nutritionist, artisan). There is a seamless synchronicity with which each one of these people arrives to work or volunteer at the charity. The right person comes at the right time with an effortlessness for which I can take no credit. This project is creating a wide circle of friends and colleagues around me that would take eons to develop if I was a stay-at-home mother in a new country.

The families we are supporting are referred by the social workers at the Children's Hospital and the triage is slow and difficult. The number of families in the programme crawls upwards so very slowly and only with great effort. I anxiously monitor these numbers, putting continuous pressure on our competent social worker to be ever-more proactive.

Each Tuesday morning, the small team of staff and large group of volunteers set up their nutrition, oral health and social assistance stations in our small rented headquarters close to the Children's Hospital. This group is made up mostly of women, with the occasional male volunteer. They are all between twenty and forty years of age. Only those over thirty have children and, although one of their children has a rare heart problem, the overall health of all of their children is good.

And then there are the families we support. Again, this group is made up of mostly women, with the occasional father participating. They are between eighteen and thirty-five years of age. All of the mothers, of course, have children, from the eighteen-year-old who left a children's home at seventeen to the thirty-five-year-old who has a young baby at home and two small children in care. All of them have children with health difficulties.

The volunteers are all educated to high school or university level and are from middle-class backgrounds. The mothers' education levels, on the other hand, are very low, with many either illiterate or functionally illiterate.

The volunteers are punctual, participate in monthly team meetings and prepare for the families – cut and prepare crafts materials, prepare donations of toothbrushes and hygiene kits, prepare healthy, organic food, research housing projects, among other activities.

The mothers are less homogenous in their behaviour. Some who have been in the programme for a few months reliably come to each meeting, but many need to be cajoled into participating – cajoled into getting the bus, which Child Health pays for – and need to be reminded of dates constantly. They often miss the meetings because of a variety of excuses, some plausible and par for the course, such as the illness of a child, but many excuses are questionable and evasive.

One day, there was a full team of ten volunteers all ready for the mothers and children and only one mother turned up. A mass of well-intentioned energy, all dressed up with nowhere to go.

There are many factors at work to make these two groups, though similar in gender and age, so different in terms of commitment, health and well-being. Beyond the different upbringings and education levels, there is a plethora of reasons, including drug abuse, income and levels of self-esteem. There is a visceral sense of abandonment of these young mothers that is day-by-day being transmitted to their children – abandonment by themselves, by their families and by public authorities.

This difference in cultures is a challenge. Keeping the volunteers engaged when family participation is unpredictable is not a challenge that I had expected. Motivating volunteers, without the tools of remuneration or extensive training opportunities, is a crash course in human nature.

Why do these volunteers give of themselves, when they receive nothing materially? And why are some of the mothers so hesitant to give of their time and effort, when they receive services, food, medicines, clothes, furniture?

It turns on its head the materialist view that receiving is more appealing than giving.

Perhaps part of the puzzle can be answered by Dr V, the founder of Child Health in Rio de Janeiro. She says that in a world of strong divisions such as Brazil, we work for social inclusion: social inclusion of the rich, as well as the poor. What she says makes sense to me. When we volunteer, we are more integrated into society; we are taking some responsibility for its more distressing situations, like the illnesses of children.

As well as the volunteers, many others are involved in Brazil, from the board members to local donors. Outside of Brazil too, so many generous people are involved through the ARCH Foundation, raising or contributing money in Ireland, the UK and the US. There is a global web of hundreds of well-wishers and supporters who are linking together to offer help to these families and children. In return, each one of us receives a sense of peace, a sense that we are doing our bit. Momentarily, we are transported beyond our own selves, beyond our self-absorbed duties, problems and pleasures. We move beyond the prison of our own ego and taste the relief and the peace it brings.

Is this peace not the best gift that can be received? Is it not better than any material or psychological offering? Rather than looking for gratitude from the families we support, perhaps we should instead offer *them* gratitude.

At the end of a Tuesday morning at Child Health Florianópolis, we all stand hand in hand, mothers, staff and volunteers, with our right palms downwards, giving energy to the person next to us and left palm upwards, receiving energy from the person next to us. The co-ordinator lets us settle into our circle for a moment and says gently, 'We hold hands and give and receive energy in this way to remember that we are never so rich or self-sufficient that we cannot receive, or so poor or vulnerable that we cannot give.'

Though our cultures may be different, we are all connected in this divine dance. It is this image of all of us, hand in hand, that is at the heart of Child Health Florianópolis' potential to transform a tiny piece of this world we live in.

Finding balance

It is June 2009 when Liam's tantrums at the classroom door start again. Both boys had settled in so well, becoming fluent in Portuguese and loving their school, friends and activities.

Liam's tantrum begins in the morning, when I drag him out of bed and sit him down to eat his breakfast. He has become, once again, the master of sabotage and he makes us later and later for school each day, by eating slowly, refusing to get dressed or brush his teeth, dragging his legs to the car. As in Oxford, I am finding that by the time I drop the children at school, I am already frazzled and exhausted. Then I head into Child Health Florianópolis and the morning races by in a plethora of tasks. The boys finish school at a quarter past twelve and I collect them and bring them home for lunch. In the afternoon, I try and finish off my work in stolen moments as I drive them to and from activities. Both boys demand time and attention from me. Tom wants me to watch him while he's playing football, not sit in the car working on the computer. Liam wants me to go into the swimming pool with him and refuses to go in alone with the teacher. There seems so much to do: the day-to-day work of the charity, which needs so much energy at this start-up stage, and the blogs and newsletters to write for the ARCH Foundation in Ireland and the UK and more board meetings to organise. And all the time there are two children to mind, feed, clothe, educate and entertain, two dogs to feed and clean up after, the house and finances to manage and the never-ending bureaucracy of passports, identity cards and visas. My mind is a continual, interminable to-do list and no matter how much I chip away at it, it never gets any shorter.

I pick the boys up from school one midday and ask for a word with the teacher, S. I am thinking of putting them into after-school care to give myself more time. I want a sympathetic ear to help me make the decision. The boys play outside while S and I sit once again on the child-size chairs.

'Liam's behaviour is becoming more and more challenging to manage,' I confide to S, 'and I simply can't get everything done that I need to do.'

S listens to me, with her hands folded neatly in her lap.

'So I think I will put them into after-school care and I can pick them up at five thirty or six when all of my work is done and I can give them my full attention for a couple of hours before I put them to bed. What do you think?'

S is silent as I finish speaking. She takes care with the words she chooses and speaks sternly. 'What do you think Liam is trying to say to you?' she asks.

I am a bit taken aback. 'What do you mean?' I retort.

'Our children come to teach us,' she says matter-of-factly. 'When Liam acts as he does, what is he trying to teach you?'

I sit back in the child-sized chair nonplussed. I genuinely

do not know what he is trying to teach me. I have been too wrapped up in what I need, what I want, to listen carefully to him.

'Think about it,' S says to me, more gently now, as she leads me out of the classroom.

I sit on this question for a few days and I watch Liam's behaviour more objectively. Now he is asking me to feed him like a baby. 'I will only eat if you feed me,' he says to me defiantly as he sits at the table with his arms crossed. I look up from the computer and notice how small he is. He is just four years old. His face still has the roundness of a baby's. He is breathtakingly beautiful with his clear blue eyes, flop of blond hair and one missing tooth. Tom comes and sits on my knee. I hold him close with one arm, as I wordlessly push the computer aside and pick up the fork to feed Liam. My two little boys, and I am the only one they have left.

As if for the first time, it dawns on me that when they lost their father, I took them away from everything that they knew – not only their large, extended family and friends, but their home, their climate, their language. When they were insecure, I uprooted them. I was so caught up in my own survival that I had not thought much about what they had needed. 'If I'm ok, they're ok' had been my mantra. I realise with each bite of food that I feed to Liam that my well-being is important for them, but only if I share it with them. Only if I am present with them – genuinely, undividedly present. That is what Liam is teaching me. Just like the stone at the Buddhist retreat after Alastair's death, Liam is trying desperately to remind me: *Be Here Now.*

That night, I lie beside Liam in bed until he falls asleep.

The next morning, I drop the children to school and call a meeting at the charity. I explain to the small team that I need to cut back the time and energy that I am giving to the organisation. 'I know this is a crucial moment, but I can only give three or four mornings a week,' I tell the team. 'It either has to work that way, or else I cannot continue.'

The nutritionist, E, who is a mother of two teenage girls, touches my arm. 'It seems like your husband made sure you would have balance in your life,' she smiles at me, 'by leaving you with two legacies: the charity project and your children.'

I smile back at her, grateful for her understanding and clear in my priorities once again.

J's visit

As I get my life into a more harmonious balance, I receive an email from J, Alastair's friend, with whom I imagined a possible relationship soon after Alastair's death. He is coming to Rio de Janeiro on business and suggests coming to Florianópolis to visit us. I am both delighted and nervous at the prospect. I email him back, reading and rereading my response several times before hitting the send button.

The boys and I go to the local airport to pick him up. 'Who is J?' Tom asks as we drive. 'He's your daddy's friend,' I tell him. 'You will recognise him when you see him.' I search my mind for some memory that will connect Tom and J. 'He came to visit us in London and he gave you chewing gum, when I said you couldn't have any.'

Tom starts to laugh. 'Now I remember,' he says happily. 'Liam, you will like J. He's fun.'

When J arrives and hugs the boys, I notice with overwhelming relief that I can see him again for who he is. He brings a sense of Alastair with him, but it is gentler than before. That evening, when the children are in bed, I sit playing backgammon with him again. He has become once more the friend that Alastair and I shared. I can truly see him, as I had before Alastair died. I see with clarity how a match between us makes little sense and I wince at my earlier desperation.

Over a beer, I clear my throat to speak with him. Equal measures of embarrassment and gratitude make me laugh nervously. I thank him for dealing so well with my advances after Alastair's death. I thank him for giving me relief from suffocating suffering. I thank him for remaining loyal to Alastair. Remembering my own fragility at the time, I thank him for letting me down gently.

'It's not because I don't love you,' he says tenderly.

I smile and refill his glass. 'In fact,' I reply, 'I think you acted as you did exactly because you *do* love me.'

We toast our friendship and get back to the game.

Generous girls

In July 2009, almost a year after we moved to Brazil, we return to Europe for our first trip home. In Ireland, I sit with my sister N, who has been leading the charge on fundraising at the ARCH Foundation. Since the moment she flew to San Francisco to be with me after Alastair's death, she has been right by my side, supporting and encouraging me every step of the way. She has already visited me in Brazil with her family, at her own expense, to see how we have settled in and to see how the work at Child Health Florianópolis is developing. She sends me a text on the twenty-seventh day of every month, the day of Alastair's death, to let me know that she is thinking of me and of Al. She bridges the chasm of my loneliness in the least-perceived moments. Alastair's death has touched her deeply. She tells me that he is the first person close to her that she has lost and it has knocked her sideways. She shares with me how much it has helped her to see life differently, to be clearer about her priorities. Where before this was harder to hear, I now feel gratitude. The undertone of what she says to me is: 'Your suffering is not in vain. Alastair's death is not in vain. Look, I am learning from it.'

As well as an incredible sister and friend, N is also a wonderful fundraiser. She seems to know everyone and is able to whip them all into action and enthusiasm to support the ARCH Foundation. She leads a committee of my friends in Ireland with a wine-sweetened iron grip, coaxing commitment after commitment from them with each wine glass she fills. She updates me now on the success of the Children's Fun Day that my other sister organised and the sponsored walk up Sugar Loaf mountain that my parents led. She shows me the photos of all my family and friends huddled together against the wind on the mountain top, drinking champagne in plastic glasses and raising a toast to Alastair. She tells me of the loud and boisterous banter at the pub quiz night, with random cash penalties for anyone seen holding an iPhone. She updates me on the samba night held in the UK in the venue where Alastair celebrated his thirtieth birthday, bringing together so many of his friends. She gives me a blow-by-blow account of the ARCH Ball they held in Dublin for 200 people.

'How did you get 200 people to pay €150 for a black-tie dinner if the country is in a bloody recession?' I ask her, gobsmacked.

'As your friend L, my co-organiser, would say,' she confides in me with a smile, 'everyone needs *a session in a recession* to chase the blues away.'

I laugh out loud.

'But it's great, Bébh,' she tells me gently. 'All of the events have been such fun and they have been as much a celebration of Alastair as fundraising events for the families in Brazil.'

I bite my lip and choke back tears.

Her eyes fill with tears too. 'And there has been some amazing out-of-the-blue generosity,' she continues. 'A lady from Mum and Dad's local church took the initiative to organise a cake sale and all the profits went to ARCH. I mean she doesn't even know you or Alastair. And a little girl of seven or eight came to the Children's Fun Day and donated €50. The lady who came with her said that the young girl had insisted on coming to the Fun Day after hearing about it on the radio. Her mother had died six months earlier and she wanted to show support to the little boys who had lost their daddy.'

Now we are both crying openly. There is so much generosity in the world. It is overwhelming. It is humbling to the core.

Final resting place

After refuelling our energies in Ireland, the boys and I take a plane to Cardiff and spend a week in my mother-in-law's holiday home in the seaside village of Mumbles in south Wales. It is shortly after the second anniversary of Alastair's death and I am finally ready to give Alastair's ashes a final resting place. On a wild and windy day in a Welsh summer, I sit with my mother-in-law on a memorial bench carved out of a tree trunk. The boys jump around us on the bench and marvel in turn at the ruin of a castle behind us and the endless ebb and flow of the sea before us. On the bench, I have engraved the following inscription to Alastair:

You are the wind in our hair,
the grass at our feet,
the mischievous grin on the faces we meet.
Thank you for all the fun and love. We love you oceans.

We stand up from the bench and pull on rain jackets to hike up one of the three cliffs near Mumbles. My mother-in-law and I walk arm in arm. I feel so much love for her and, through her, for Alastair. High above the ever-expanding ocean and the curves of the bay, she opens a bottle of champagne to celebrate Alastair's memory, as the boys run around in the wind, flapping their arms like birds about to take flight. As I watch her, I notice a frailty in her that I have never seen before. She is in her mid-seventies and has always been very thin, but she had seemed so unbreakably strong and independent to me before. A few months after Alastair's death, however, she suffered her first stroke. She has recovered well, almost completely it seems, but Alastair's death has dealt a fatal blow to her vitality.

I take the dark-brown wooden box of Alastair's ashes out of my bag. I move my fingers one last time across the smooth gold-painted nameplate and trace the curves of his name and the date of his death. I sit with the box at the cliff edge and call the boys to me. They run at me, burying their faces into my neck to escape the wind. 'We love you, Daddy,' I call as I open the box of ashes and scatter them over the cliffs. The wind whips the ashes away, with some blowing back into my face. I shelter the boys from both the wind and the grey ash of their father's remains.

I shake the ash from my face, but some sticks to the moisture of my lips. I lick my lips slowly, carefully imbibing the last of Alastair's body. There I sit at the cliff edge with the boys clinging to me. We shake from a mixture of cold and emotion, watching Alastair's body become the wind in our hair.

Friendly welcome

After a month in Europe, the boys and I return to Brazil. We are met at the airport by W and I notice my pleasure at seeing him. The boys run into his arms and laugh as he swings them playfully. We had very little contact during my month away. There is a freedom and a lack of commitment to this relationship that is new to me.

The first day that W came to visit us in our little house in Santo Antônio de Lisboa, he had entered the kitchen and stood for a few minutes in silence with his eyes closed. He appeared to be praying. When he'd opened his eyes, he smiled at me.

'What were you doing?' I had asked intrigued.

'I was blessing your home,' he had said, 'and I was telling Alastair that as long as I am with you and the boys, I will not do you any harm.'

I had beamed at him and hugged him closely. This is just

what I need. A caretaker for me and the boys; a caretaker for Alastair's family.

W and I are getting closer to each other. He is the perfect boyfriend for me right now. He has no expectations and makes few demands. He graciously accepts what is offered, when he wants it. He offers me only that which he is happy to give. He is neither a husband nor a father, but he is becoming a great friend to the boys and to me. He is my new best friend with benefits, my 'colourful friend' as they say here in Brazil.

I watch myself as I endlessly, callously compare him to Alastair in every aspect. I know that living up to my now untainted image of Alastair is an impossible task, but nevertheless I mercilessly relegate W to second place. W does not seem to mind. He has more self-esteem than anyone I have ever met. He truly likes himself and does not suffer from others' perceptions of him. He does not bend to meet anyone's expectations. This is so new to me and it makes me miss even more my attentive, accommodating husband. It is also freeing. Why, then, am I feeling so afraid?

Part of me would love to immerse myself again in the life of a man. Part of me would love to believe again that a man could give me security and certainty. But I cannot unknow what I have come to know. I cannot believe in a security that I know viscerally does not exist and W will certainly not entertain illusions.

Together in a new way

At the end of October, on the day that would have been Alastair's and my eighth wedding anniversary, Tom and I are in the car driving to his football lesson. I stop the car to greet a neighbour briefly and Tom laughs at me from his booster seat in the back. As we drive away, he squeals at me, 'Mummy, you sound so funny.'

When we first arrived in Brazil, the boys did not speak one word of Portuguese and I was the 'fluent' one. How quickly this has been reversed. Now, over a year after we arrived, the boys switch from English to Portuguese so smoothly, so naturally. Their Brazilian accent is native and mine is caught in an eternal *gringa* lilt. Now they often laugh at my accent and odd turn-of-phrase, pointing out all my mistakes and mispronunciations mercilessly. I joke with them and sigh in contentment. Alastair and I always wanted this early bilingualism for the boys and they have taken to it beautifully.

Earlier that day, I picked the boys up from school and, when I met them, each one handed me a Happy Anniversary card. I love that they make these cards and that they make cards for Father's Day and Alastair's birthday. I love that they hand the cards they make to me with no hint of sorrow or loss. Mummy takes care of Daddy's cards for him. Simple, no drama.

As we arrive at the football pitch, Tom jumps out of the car and runs towards a group of boys. He is wearing his football club uniform, which is a bit too big for him, and his shiny new football boots. In an afterthought, he turns and waves at me. I am watching him through the open window as he waves and a thought rises quickly, grabbing me by my throat. *If only Alastair was here to see this.* I am swallowed by an unexpected sense of grief about how much Alastair is missing. About how many things I cannot share with him and how many things the boys are missing without even knowing it. I am undone by the force of these thoughts.

My mind goes automatically back to 'The Work', which has become more and more natural for me when a painful thought strikes. 'Wait a second,' I hear the calm part of myself tell my soap-opera self, 'without the thought that Alastair isn't here to share this moment, how would this moment be?' I look back at Tom and notice how beautiful he is, how full of life his little face is. I am missing his beauty by being caught up in these thoughts.

My inner monologue continues: 'Can you know that it's true? Can you know that Alastair isn't with you?' My mind goes back to my dreams of Alastair, my occasional sense of his presence. I look at my face in the rear-view mirror and for the tiniest of seconds I am Alastair looking back at me.

What if Alastair is here somehow? What if he is sharing this moment and every moment? A blessing from Alastair's funeral, that has lain dormant in the recesses of my mind, blows through me:

Alastair, may the blessing of Bébhinn, Tom and Liam and all your family be with you in a new way, as your whole family embraces each other within God's wide embrace of us all.

Is it possible that we are still together, not as before but in another, more subtle way? How frustrating for Alastair to be enjoying his son in his new football outfit and to have it tainted by my lack of awareness, my inability to sense him.

Look at Tom. He is not upset. He is showing me one more time that life happens now, right now, and it is complete as it is, not as it *should* be or *could have* been.

I wave back to Tom, lighter now, bursting with love for him and for Alastair. I am a bridge between them; Alastair sees Tom through me.

Unconditional love

Later that evening, I am sitting alone on the terrace of our house in Florianópolis with a glass of red wine, toasting our wedding anniversary and reliving Alastair's and my relationship. As I go chronologically through the images in my mind, I feel calm for the most part about how we spent our seven years. We took full advantage of our time together, moving abroad and becoming home to each other, travelling to over twenty countries and marrying in a wonderful, romantic ceremony surrounded by family and friends. We shared the first years of parenthood together and still laughed together and made love. We went on trips away without the children and made time for our own relationship. When he came home from work, he still kissed me first before cooing over the day's discoveries and achievements of his young sons.

As I sip my wine, only one regret needles me: I did not accept Alastair totally as he was. I tried to change him, especially telling him to leave his job and do something that fulfilled him completely. I wanted him to follow his passion, but not purely because I thought that would make him happy. I had never seen myself as someone who would marry the company man. I wanted him to be more alternative, more of a risk-taker. I wanted him to be more present too. I did not want to have the dregs of him, when he finally got home late in the evening. I wanted him to give the bulk of his energy to me, to the boys, to his family and friends, and not to his job. When I think now of the time I wasted, tut-tutting his work and feeling jealous of his long hours, I wish I could have simply accepted him. My love would have been purer had I loved him completely as he was and not wasted his and my energy trying to change him.

I feel a rising frustration that I cannot share this insight with Alastair anymore. It is too late. I flush with envy of those whose spouse has a health scare or diagnosis of a drawn-out disease that leaves time for them to say and do all that they want before death. Unlike Alastair and me, they have time to be jolted into full presence in their love.

As I fill my glass again, it suddenly dawns on me that I can in fact still use this insight of unconditional love with Alastair. He is dead and I am wishing him to be different. I am wishing for him to be alive. Once again I am not loving him 100 per cent as he is. For some reason that I do not understand, Alastair has to be dead now. He has to be, because he is. I have the chance to accept his death and love him dead, rather than willing him to impossible life, causing increased suffering in me and maybe even in him. It is not too late to use this insight of unconditional love on him.

I close my eyes and call him to me. This time, though, I do not try and conjure an image of him alive, joking and moving towards me. I imagine him instead as a spirit, peaceful and calm before me. I imagine my heart showering his spirit with love, not just accepting but loving that he is where he needs to be.

Compassion

The first anniversary of Child Health Florianópolis is upon us. It is 6 December 2009 and I have taken the boys with me to the celebrations. I involve the boys in the charity whenever I can, bringing them to all the fundraising events and to visit the headquarters from time to time. They ask endless questions about the children and their illnesses, about their homes and their needs, many of which I cannot answer. Often when they get presents of money from relatives, they hand it to me, informing me that half of it is for Daddy's charity. I hope this experience makes them more aware of how fortunate they are and more sensitive and compassionate to others. Most keenly though, I hope that through seeing this work we have created in their father's name, they know viscerally how much I and all his family and friends love him. I hope that the effort we all make to honour Alastair and further his good work demonstrates to his sons in a tangible way the kind of man he was.

As I watch the boys bounce on a trampoline on the beach with children from the programme, a thought clarifies in my mind. It strikes me that by opening up to the avalanche of suffering after Alastair's death, I have been rewarded with a perfect round pearl that sits dainty and priceless in the cup of my hand. As I look closer, I see a word form in the misty white of the pearl. The word is 'compassion'. It is a brand-new emotion for me: not an 'us and them' pity or sadness, but the sharing of suffering. When I had walked the halls of Stanford Hospital after Alastair's death, I had my first taste of the heartbreaking beauty of experiencing death up close. The experience with the families of Child Health Florianópolis has led this cracked-open heart into new territory.

I used to live as if the objective of life was to get through it with as little suffering as possible. I gauged to see how well I was doing by comparing myself with those around me. After Alastair's death, I compare myself between two extremes: the lives of the families in the charity in Brazil and those of my friends back home in Ireland and England.

Looking at the lives of the families that the charity encounters brings my own everyday worries into sharp perspective. Feeling down over the frustrating monotony and stubbornness of the endless to-do list appears somewhat ridiculous when another mother is struggling to feed her children properly or being told her child has lost a kidney. On telling a friend in Oxford of my plans to come to Brazil, she noted how helpful it would be to encounter people who were suffering more than me. The sentiment took me aback. The idea of finding comfort in other people's suffering is an uneasy one for me. Perhaps at the time, the idea that anything would ever make me feel genuinely better was also an uneasy one, laced with incredulity and a low-humming guilt.

When I sit in Florianópolis, in my solid, fire-heated house on nights of cold winds and torrential rain, I do feel a sense of gratitude and relief that my boys and I are not in M's shoes. M is one of the mothers in the programme, who has AIDS and two children with HIV and lives in a wooden house that would be regarded as nothing more than a shoddy tree house back home. So, yes, there is some sense that others' material suffering does help me to appreciate the material well-being that Alastair's years of hard work have ensured for the boys and me. I acknowledge also the sense of recognition I felt when I met C, a mother who has gone through the programme in Rio de Janeiro and has faced the challenges of her son's sudden severe illness, an abusive husband and limited education. There was a voice in me that reassured me, 'You are not alone, others suffer too; you are not the only one cast out by the gods.' There was comfort in this sense of shared suffering.

At times I tried to deny the validity of my own suffering. Years before my tears were sufficiently shed, I had told myself that I had no real right to feel pain. 'My suffering is nothing in the big scheme of things,' I said to my friend L, 'at least I can still take care of my children and have enough money to eat and live.'

She turned to me with annoyance, speaking from experience. 'I don't care how rich or poor you are,' she said tightly, 'losing someone you love is one of the hardest things to endure in life.'

Her words and tone marked me.

Before I went to Brazil, my friend S sat opposite me and raised a toast to me with a glass of red wine. 'May your suffering open up a bridge to understanding and compassion for the suffering of others.'

I clinked her glass, unaware of how prophetic her words would be. By sharing and expressing my own experience of suffering, many of those around me begin to show their frailties too. Language barriers, social class barriers, age barriers are all broken down in the sharing of suffering.

My trip home to Ireland and England brought me face to face with the difficulties of comparisons in the other direction.

Holidaying with a group of lovely friends and my huge, wonderful family was sometimes difficult for me. Most of them seemed to continue in the bustle of two-point-four children and a stable relationship in the land of happily-ever-after. This intensified my own awareness of the meteoric implosion of my own happily-ever-after through Alastair's sudden death. Feelings of *why Alastair?*, *why me?* and, perhaps most painfully and incessantly, *why our two little boys?* rose and fell like waves of the icy Irish Sea. At times, I did find discomfort in others' lack of suffering.

As I remember the feelings of injustice that ripped through me and become aware of my own reaction and guilt at these feelings, I begin to hear the whisper of another truth. It is a low, calm voice that, over the years, has become laced with Alastair's own steady tone. This voice tells me that one scratch under the flimsy surface will show that everyone has a tale of difficulty and challenge to tell. As I look beyond my easy envy of those still in the world of happily-ever-after, I find friends who are separating, who cannot conceive, whose children have serious illnesses, who have suffered abuse, who face life-threatening diseases. And beyond that, when I truly lower the lenses of my 'poor-me' pettiness, I begin to notice that genuinely happy people are hard to come by. People, including me, suffer from a myriad of internal tortures: their sense of inadequacy, the fear of their own mortality, their monumental and everyday losses.

Suffering is shared but between all of us, whether in Ireland or England, Rwanda or Brazil, whether rich or poor, whether caused by poverty, the illness of a child, the death of a loved one, divorce, or by the simple and unforgiving recognition of our own human weaknesses and limitations. All but the enlightened few suffer, to varying, uncategorisable degrees. I silently mouth the word 'compassion' again and taste its newness. My compassion begins to embrace all people, including myself.

Like the bulb on the Christmas lights that is finally screwed on properly, I am flushed with light at my own suffering, and simultaneously the whole chain of humanity, and my place in it, is illuminated for me.

Choosing peace

Brazil is gradually becoming home to us. The work in Alastair's name is going well. The children are doing well. I am doing well. It is the fertile ground on which the seeds of peace from the Byron Katie retreat are beginning to push through and blossom. One warm winter's day, almost two years after we arrived in Brazil, we go for a walk on our favourite secluded beach. The boys run on ahead of me, stopping from time to time to pick up crumbling sand dollars or point out the lifeless crusts of sea urchins and crabs. Tom finds a tiny seahorse that has been washed up on the beach and excitedly calls us to look. These are the moments I know that the boys are in the right place, living a free, carefree childhood, immersed in awe-inspiring nature. After examining the seahorse closely, Tom hands it over to me ceremoniously on an open palm. Then the two boys tear off down the beach to inspect the catch in a fisherman's bucket, as he deftly throws his tarrafa net into the shallow waters of the sea with a fluid flick of his wrist. The moisture on the net is caught in the rays of the low afternoon sun and shimmers in the air for a moment before it falls.

I place the seahorse slowly and carefully in my pocket. My hand rubs against a smooth, flat pebble that my friend S gave to me after Alastair died. I often keep this pebble with me and in random moments I caress its velvet-smooth contours and mull over its inscription. On one side of the pebble it says: 'Everything happens for a reason.' On the other side, it says: 'Just believe.'

I think about how Alastair would have taken it and skimmed it skilfully along the surface of a calm sea, whooping with pleasure as it jumped five or six times.

My mind goes back to the week after his death. At the time, I had repeated to my sister-in-law, 'This is the worst thing that could happen, the worst thing that could happen.'

I had stacked Alastair's death up in my overly busy mind against every other possible disaster in my life and it ranked first. I had believed Alastair was a victim to die at thirty-nine. I had felt Tom and Liam were victims to be left without such a great father at their young ages. I had felt an acute poor-me victimhood at being left with two small children and a broken heart, spinning without direction. What was lost was not only the vibrancy of my laughing, loving, supportive, frustrating life-sparring partner who had shared my every day; not only the adoring, childlike father for our little boys; not only the cheeky apple of my mother-in-law's eye, but everything in me too: my belief in life and its goodness and its simple symmetry. I had been nauseous, too, with the bitter-tasting wastefulness of his death, the waste of such an intelligent and competent man who seemed on the brink of contributing so much more to the world.

At the time, my brother had tried to reassure me that Alastair's death was not a tragedy. 'He was born, had children and died,' he had said. 'He did as much as we are all put here to do.'

I had let these words sink in and rejected them. Such a reductionist view of life does no justice to Alastair or to any of us. We are not animals merely multiplying our species. I now remember Alastair's eight-year-old niece and goddaughter had bemoaned after the funeral, 'If only he had lived ten more years.'

I had replied with automatic intuition, 'And what if he had lived ten less years, missing out on being your godfather, on having his two sons, on marrying me?'

As I stand now, looking out on the vastness of the ocean before me, it begins to truly dawn on me that it is the way I think about Alastair's death that defines it as a tragedy or not, at least for me. The seeds planted at the Byron Katie retreat are beginning to bear fruit. What if Alastair had fulfilled his true life's mission unbeknownst to me, unbeknownst to himself? What if his death had been a form of promotion, more true and ambitious than his promotion at work? What if he had lived just enough time and had done just enough of everything? What if nothing had been wasted, but his life had been all that it was meant to be in content and length? What if, indeed, his death had been part of my essential journey on earth too? And the boys, what if their father's death had been part of their path too – necessary for them to grow and evolve as they need? What if his death had happened *for* us and not *to* us?

Giving space to the possibility of these thoughts brings me a great sense of peace and humility.

I am at a crossroads.

One path is paved with our victimhood – a path that will allow me to use Alastair's death as a reason to be unhappy, unfulfilled and an excuse to demand that others take care of me and the boys for the rest of our lives. Just like Tom in the Tesco queue, I could use Alastair's death for the rest of my life as a story which would enable me to grab on to the always-coveted attention that my ego longs for.

It is tempting. It attracts me with its passivity. It releases me from being responsible for my own happiness. When I trip a few steps down this road, however, I realise that it leads only to bitterness and to unfair expectations and demands on others. Most of all though, there is no laughter. I ache for real belly laughter back in my life.

The other path is less clear. It is the path of taking responsibility for my own suffering and for my own happiness. It is the path pointed out to me on the retreat, with the clear understanding that it is not what happens to me in life that defines how happy or sad I am, but what I believe about it. As I peer down this path tentatively, it twists to the unimaginable.

Time after time, I have found myself at this crossroads. Here I am again, mustering all vestiges of courage within me to take the second path. It has taken more than three years of pain-alleviating busyness and reflection to get here. It has taken the generous support of my family and friends, of counsellors and spiritual retreats. It has taken an open heart, a surrender to the emotions and experiences that Alastair's death unleashed. It has taken an overriding desire to live fully, to laugh all of my laughter.

I cannot help feeling that some invisible friend has had a hand in it, be it Alastair's spirit or God or life itself. As I choose this second path, I gradually feel the dark cloud lift from my life. I begin to see the potential that life holds for me to be happy again. The future beckons now and the unknown is no longer menacing. I begin to count all of my blessings again, not just those that idealise my life with Alastair. Maybe my brother is right in one way. Maybe Alastair's death was not a tragedy. Not because he procreated. Nor because he achieved the potential others projected onto him. But because when I believe it is a tragedy, I create victims and I focus on what is lost.

When I believe that Alastair's death is not a tragedy, I focus on the fact that his life was a gift: to him, to me, to his children and all who loved him. It allows his memory to breathe within me. It brings him back to life for me – the Alastair that made me laugh; the Alastair that could whip me out of a bad mood in under a minute; the Alastair that got so excited about the smallest things in life, joking with friends about their foibles, drinking a cold beer as the sun set, lost in shared laughter with Tom and Liam.

When I do not focus on what is lost, I see clearly that I am lucky to have my two healthy boys, endless support from family and friends, and enough money to be able to bring up the boys without financial headaches and to offer them a host of opportunities. I understand too that Alastair was lucky that he had such a great life, with all of the love, travel and adventure that he crammed into it. I appreciate with gratitude that Liam and Tom are lucky to be born out of so much love and lucky that their father lived long enough to have both of them so that they have each other.

One friend comforted me by saying that we are lucky to have experienced the love and life we shared. 'Most people,' she added wistfully, 'never get a chance to live that.'

I realise that every moment of our seven years together is not lost and neither death nor time can rob us of it: the casual 'live a little' that Alastair winked at me the day before he died when we went on the carousel without paying; the magic of a family of four laughingly dabbing ice-cream cones on each other's noses; the fluttering moment of recognising mutual love. These memories are part of me still. None of this is lost. These moments are accessible at the turn of a photograph or through a favourite song on the radio or in a moment of quiet reflection.

As I let go of the oppressive thoughts that Alastair's death was a tragedy, that he, the boys and I are victims, that all is lost, I am filled with a growing sense of peace.

As my eyes open, truly open, I even glimpse what has been gained through Alastair's death. It is hard to admit that there are positive aspects to a life after Alastair's death, even to myself, but I realise that accepting the good that has come from Alastair's death allows me to live with hope and a sense of purposeful beauty in the world.

This starts with small things. I love having breakfast in bed, but Alastair hated it, complaining of crumbs on the sheets that attracted ant trails. In our seven years together, I very rarely had breakfast in bed. Now I start to have breakfast in bed again and allow myself to enjoy it. With the boys, I find myself becoming more myself with them, rather than taking on the more traditional mother role, complemented by Alastair's fun father role. I am freed from the societal norms on the father–mother divide in parenting and can choose which role and activities are most authentically mine.

Despite the uncertainty and loneliness, I can see that my life situation has been blown open into a new freedom. I am now freer to live my life exactly as I want to, without having to compromise to fit Alastair's career, plans or priorities. I can do anything and go anywhere I want to. I do not think, for example, that Alastair and I would have gone to live in Florianópolis, as his career would have been tied to big cities.

The boys too are gaining from the experience of his death. They are being brought up bilingually and tri-culturally, opening a whole world of diverse life experiences for them. Alastair's death led us directly to Florianópolis and to a Waldorf education, which is nurturing every aspect of them with an emphasis on their spiritual growth. If Alastair was still alive, it is highly unlikely that they would have had that opportunity. They are also being confronted by death and breaking its terrorising spell at such an early age. From the beginning of their own conscious lives, they are aware of the transience and tenuousness of physical life, which may awaken them to appreciate each moment, each day that they are granted. They have gained a close familiarity with death and know first hand its limit: it cannot kill love, the most perennial of all things.

I remember a scene from Oxford. As I cried, slumped up against the oven as the boys ate their tea, a four-year-old Tom had told me in an exasperated little voice, 'Don't cry, Mummy, remember, it's only his body that died.' These boys are growing up with an intimate understanding of their spiritual nature that eludes most people for lifetimes.

If someone offered me a choice, I would jump in a heartbeat at having Alastair back, at embracing again both the richness and the compromise of shared living. However, despite my negotiations with God, this choice no longer exists. Nothing, not even a lifetime of suffering, will bring him back. Sometimes I almost fall back into equating suffering with love, but how can that be true? If I suffer with Alastair's death for the rest of my life, I will hand down that suffering to our children like a ghastly family heirloom that will suck the life out of them like an eternal leech. How could I want that? How could Alastair want that?

If I suffer for the rest of my life, Alastair will have enabled me only seven years of joy and (possibly) decades of pain. How can that be? How can he be an overall negative influence on my life? That is the direct opposite of how he was while alive, the direct opposite of how I want to remember him.

My life with Alastair by my side has died and my options now are either to live in the shadow of that life or embrace this new life, this new reality. Like everything, his death has both negative and positive consequences. I have wallowed long enough in the negative. I know them, I live them, I accept them. Courage is opening up to the positive too. Courage is listening to my visceral gut-feel that life is good.

Maybe the reason for Alastair's death is that he had done all he needed to do, including dying when he did. Maybe one reason for his death was to enable the boys and me to continue on our paths to grow and evolve as we need. Maybe his life and death were not just enough, but were in fact an abundance.

I choose to be a traitor to misery. I choose to 'just believe'.

Love, a ford and laughter

Florianópolis is indeed the island of magic, as the locals say, and it has been weaving its magic into the fabric of my heart for over two and a half years. It is called the island of magic because women accused of practising witchcraft were exiled from Europe and sent here at the time of the Portuguese colonisation in the mid-eighteenth century. Today, the *benzedeiras*, or spiritual women, can still be found on the island and are sought out by locals in times of difficulty. Legend has it is that the seventh child has this potential spiritual gift. When people ask me why I came to Brazil, I tell them about the charity and my dream of Alastair calling me here. When they ask me why I came specifically to Florianópolis, I am not so sure of the answer. Echoing a sentiment of Fr D, my enlightened Catholic priest from Ireland, I would say that signs led me here. I find meaning in the idea that, as the seventh child in my family, the island of magic called me.

One afternoon, as the children play *frescobol* in the garden and I sit on our terrace, enthralled by a humming bird flirting with a red hibiscus flower, I am filled with a soaring sense of gratitude. It is clear to me that I am a flower like any other. I spend most of my life in the mud. Alastair's death, however, has helped me to begin to pull myself from the mud and to blossom. I have suffered, but the calm voice within me, strengthened through Alastair's death, whispers that it is what I do with my suffering that is most important. It suggests that through suffering, I have the chance to break open and grow, to embrace life with splashes of passion and courage that cannot be bought in self-help books or advanced philosophy or psychology degrees. When I think back on the families in the charity and on many friends and family members, I recognise not only that they suffer, but their ability to survive it. In a few inspiring cases, I see that some have blossomed from the darkness of their suffering.

For me, the bud that is forming from the experience, suffering and consequences of Alastair's death is a new embryonic spiritual awakening in me. After Alastair's death, I am freefalling and I am overwhelmed with a sense of fear and freedom. The fear is my mind losing false certainties and the freedom is an emerging song of my soul.

When Alastair and I married, I engraved our wedding rings with the Irish words for 'love, luck and laughter'. I made a mistake in the spelling though and wrote a *t* instead of a *d* in the Irish word for luck. This changed the meaning of the word. Instead of 'luck' ('ádh'), the word now translates as 'ford' ('áth'), a piece of land that helps you cross from one side of a river to another. A friend pointed this out to Alastair and me on the eve of our wedding. Alastair guffawed loudly, 'Great job, my love! We will now have a life full of love, *a ford* and laughter.' After his death, the thought momentarily crossed my mind that maybe this mistake was the cause of our absence of luck in a marriage cut so short.

It strikes me now, however, that perhaps Alastair is indeed a ford to me; a ford leading me from an earlier life of beautiful bullshit to a more expansive experience of life.

The beautiful bullshit is the belief that I can nimbly dodge suffering while following the 'Game of Life' which spans from happy childhood to genuine adolescent friendships, to university degrees, to rewarding career and contributions to those less fortunate, to lifelong love and marriage, to easily conceived, healthy and successful children, to travelling the world, and finally to death in old age. It is the addictive fairytale I used to spin myself of guaranteed lifelong marriage and purchasable insurance against illness and death and devastating heartbreak. It is the childish fable of 'if I work hard and treat people well and make a contribution, I will be safe from suffering'.

Alastair's sudden death brings me face to face with the transience of life. I am overwhelmed with the deep realisation of my own mortality and my fragile hold on life. I remember a friend referring to the palpable sense of shock among the hundreds of people at Alastair's funeral. This large group of mostly young and middle-aged friends and family had been saddened by Alastair's loss, by our family's loss, but they had not seemed to connect it to themselves. There had been an invisible but clear line between the unlucky (Alastair) and the lucky (them). My friend had then compared it with her father-in-law's recent funeral. He had died from illness in his mid-sixties and the funeral had been awash with his contemporaries. At that funeral, she'd confided in me, the atmosphere had been totally different. He was the first of the group to die. There had been sadness at his death, of course, but there had been a visceral sense of dread and foreboding too. Now in their sixties themselves, they had recognised that his fate was also their inevitable fate. The question, 'Will I be next?' had hung heavy in the air.

For me, there is no invisible line between Alastair and all the rest of us. Alastair's death is so close, I can feel the heat of its breath on the nape of my neck. He brings death to my rumpled bedsheets, to the creases of our children's double buggy. His death makes the fact that my parents will die, my children will die, I will die real and tangible to me. The bell is tolling for me and I am living in the shadow of death. Questions ring endlessly within me: *Where were we running to in life with all our busyness and frenzied activity?* Surrounded by Alastair's clothes and belongings, swimming in the debris of the stubs from his salary, his box of sports medals, his academic certificates, I had screamed out loud, 'What do we take with us? What is it from this life that remains when we die?'

Alastair's death and the questions it has unleashed forge a ford between this earlier shore of beautiful bullshit to a new shore of more clarity and more awareness of my physical transience and my true spiritual nature. It is a path on which I am taking tiny, baby steps.

This new shore is a subtle certainty that we are spiritual beings having a mortal experience and not mortal beings having groggy, spiritual experiences at nine thirty mass on a Sunday morning. I recall the Buddhist retreat I went on after Alastair's death and remember the words of the monk who told us that meditation is a way of life, not an add-on hobby to a busy life. I begin to understand. I have had everything upside down. Meditation is the way of life, spirituality is my true nature. It is the busy life that is the add-on.

I read endlessly of death. I am hugely comforted by books on near-death experiences, which relate similar experiences across cultures, across religions, across age groups. So many people speak of a sense of overwhelming peace and of a spiritual continuation. I relish the idea that I will meet Alastair again. I remember the strong magnetic pull I felt towards him when I was getting to know him and I know deep within myself that it was a type of recognition. Even if we are not in the same physical forms when we meet again, I know that this magnetic recognition will reveal him to me.

I am propelled towards a direct relationship with God, bypassing religious hierarchy and dogma to light a fire of joy and divine recognition within me. This is where Byron Katie's 'The Work' and Osho and his dynamic meditations are pointing – towards the divine in me.

I remember the prophetic dreams, the changing sense of Alastair's state of being after his death, the synchronicities that led me to Brazil and towards the realisation of our dreams. I remember my request for true love all those years ago on the Way of St James and one of the passages from Kahlil Gibran's *The Prophet* comes to mind:

For even as love crowns you so shall he crucify you.
Even as he is for your growth so is he for your pruning.
All these things shall love do unto you that you may know
the secrets of your heart, and in that knowledge become a
fragment of Life's heart.

I am the witness of life answering my own prayers.

I remember my elating experience of grace in Oxford and how it evoked in me the sense of egoless love, so similar to my feeling for Alastair. If (what we call) God's love is truly light years beyond our human love, than perhaps this sensation is but a taste of what awaits me in embracing a spiritual life with more meditation and mindfulness. Perhaps it is just a tiny taste of the joy and peace that awaits us all in death.

My close friend, I, who lives in Brazil, rings me out of the blue to tell me she is coming to Florianópolis on a week-long spiritual retreat and we arrange to meet before she flies back home. When we meet in a restaurant near the airport, I am struck by her visible joy and the sense of lightness and love that surrounds her.

'What kind of retreat have you been on?' I ask, intrigued.

'Oh, Bébhinn,' she smiles at me, 'there is an enlightened master just an hour from your house. He was Osho's bodyguard for many years in India and became enlightened after spending time alone in the Himalayas after Osho's death.' She adds, 'All of the retreats and meetings with him are in English as well as Portuguese.'

My heart leaps. How convenient life is, I smile to myself. Who would have thought that an enlightened follower of my mystic guide Osho would be holding retreats one hour away from my new home in Brazil, in English? Synchronicity, once more, is showing me the way.

Life is calling me to take time into my true self. A more open, more authentic path rises up to meet me and I am reignited by its spark.

A circle closing

On a warm spring night in 2011, three years after we arrived in Brazil, I am driving my car illegally up a street in the centre of Florianópolis. Night has fallen and I have finally, finally found a parking spot for my car. I position my car between two other randomly parked cars on this pedestrian street, right next to the imposing cathedral.

I am late.

I glance quickly at my reflection in the rear-view mirror for a last look at myself. I am a mess. I ran out of the house half an hour earlier, detaching tired, moaning children from my body as I left, my friend C assuring me they would be fine. I had no time for a shower before throwing on a colourful skirt and grabbing a woollen, hooded top to warm me against the slight chill in the night air. I am wearing no make-up, my hair is barely combed and I have a red sore right under my nose, where I had hit myself against the car door earlier in the day. I sigh, open the door and run towards my destination, the Álvaro de Carvalho Theatre, at the top of the street.

The whole area is heaving with parked cars. There are bright lights and music coming from the theatre. I run up the marble steps, panting. Two tuxedoed bodyguards move closer to block me from running straight inside. 'Are you one of the candidates?' they ask dubiously.

I stop to look up at them. 'I am,' I say to them, suddenly feeling intimidated and out of place. They hand me a sticker for my lapel and move aside to let me in.

The theatre lies grandiose before me. Gentle, welcoming lighting ushers me forward into the anteroom. Glamorous women in their finery waft from side to side. An air of perfectly manicured elegance accompanies them. Agh, nobody told me it was black tie! I breathe deeply, smoothing down my creased peacock skirt. I follow the muffled sounds of laughing chatter and piped background music into the main theatre. The stage rises up large before me, with a string quartet preparing to play at its centre. I look around for my colleague T from Child Health Florianópolis who is keeping a seat for me. She waves at me from the third row and I walk up hurriedly to sit beside her. Just as I sit down, the quartet begins to play and a silence hushes over the crowd. *Thank goodness the Brazilians lack punctuality as much as I do,* I think to myself, trying to quieten my heavy breathing.

The MC, a beautiful, well-groomed blonde woman, stands by the podium. 'Welcome to Florianópolis' annual awards ceremony for Women Who Make a Difference. Let us all stand for the Brazilian national anthem.'

I notice contentedly that the one woman in the quartet is a volunteer at Child Health Florianópolis, and had played at our annual fundraiser earlier in the year.

The awards ceremony is organised by Florianópolis's high-profile Industry and Commerce Association. I have been coerced by T into leaving the children and coming along. In between the quartet's tasteful repertoire of classical music, the presidents of different branches of the association make short speeches to the crowd. The MC briefly presents the forty-seven candidates and their work and pays customary homage to local politicians, philanthropists and successful business professionals. There will be one prize awarded in each category: the public sector, the commercial sector and the charity sector. Ten anonymous judges have independently rated each of the candidates' achievements and the barriers they overcame to make them.

I watch as my photo appears on the screen above the stage and the beautiful blonde stumbles over my name. 'This candidate has come from Ireland to honour her deceased husband in setting up

Child Health Florianópolis,' she summarises, before moving on to the next candidate.

I twist uncomfortably in my chair. Once again, I feel out of place. I watch as a familiar battle plays out within me. My culturally ingrained aversion to showiness and self-promotion wrestles scathingly with a more gracious acceptance of external recognition.

As they name the three finalists in each group, I am surprised to hear my name among them. I do not know if it is modesty that makes me blush as they call me to the stage or a hesitance to take personal credit for a collective effort. I walk awkwardly onto the stage with the three other finalists in my sector and receive a bunch of flowers. When requested, I turn to the photographers and give something between a smile and a wince.

The three of us are asked to leave the stage and I sigh in relief, almost tripping down the stairs as I move.

Back in my seat, the finalists in the public and commercial sectors are announced and two tall, well-dressed women take their awards and make short, forceful speeches, each one overflowing with self-confidence.

Now it is time to name the winner in the charity sector. To the backdrop of Vivaldi's 'Spring', the MC stumbles over the name of the winner and immediately I know: I have won.

My jaw dives floor-bound in surprise. It takes me a few seconds to compose myself, before I grab on to the back of the chair before me, pull myself to a stand, walk to the stairs and climb up to the stage.

I accept the applause and the congratulations. I accept the tasteful trophy with my name engraved on it. Somehow, I do not feel a hint of nerves.

I look down at the audience. The theatre is full before me. Many of Florianópolis' wealthy families are represented, including many successful business professionals and a handful of politicians. I see my colleague T and in my seat, Dr M is sitting and beaming up at me, applauding. I had not known she was in the audience and I am filled with pleasure at her presence.

'It is proof of how international Florianípolis is that a *gringa* could win this prize,' I begin and there is gentle laughter in the crowd.

I clear my throat. 'I would like to thank everyone involved in this award,' I continue, 'and tell you that I am very surprised to receive it. In the audience here, I have seen several people from different charities who have worked tirelessly for many years to provide support to people in need in Florianópolis. It is an honour to be in their presence and receive this award representing Child Health Florianópolis, an organisation that is at the beginning of its journey. Although Child Health Florianópolis is important for the children and families that it serves, it is a grain of sand in a desert of need.'

A quotation that a speaker had mentioned at the beginning of the ceremony comes to my mind. It is from the Brazilian poet Cora Coralina: '*I am the woman who climbed the mountain of life, clearing away stones and planting flowers.*'

'I enjoyed the quotation from Cora Coralina earlier,' I share with the audience, 'and it strikes me that Child Health Florianópolis is the result of an effort to clear away stones and plant flowers. When I was thirty-one, my husband, Alastair Ramsay, died suddenly, when our youngest son was just one year old. This was a gigantic stone that fell across my path. Since his death, I have been trying to clear away this stone and plant flowers in its place. Child Health Florianópolis is one of these flowers. And I am not the only woman who has been doing this. Here, tonight, are the co-founders Dr M and T.' I point them out in the crowd and hearty applause ensues. 'Hundreds of women in Brazil, England, Ireland, America have helped to plant this flower. This is a collective, not a personal effort. So many volunteers have been involved. There is even one on stage right now.' I point now to the violinist in the quartet, who smiles up at me. The audience laughs audibly, surprised, and applauds her. The presence of all the volunteers, staff, fundraisers and contributors of the ARCH Foundation and Child Health Florianópolis is palpable to me and this applause extends to all of them.

'We even have some fine men involved in this effort,' I say laughing. 'In fact, although I am receiving an award for the Woman Who Makes a Difference, my part in Child Health Florianópolis should be attributed to a man. I did this work in my husband's name.' My voice begins to break. 'And,' I stammer, 'and I would like to take this opportunity to thank him.'

The crowd applauds him.

'At the heart of Child Health Florianópolis are the mothers, each of whom is dealing with poverty and their child's illness. Each one of these women is trying to clear away the many stones in their paths and Child Health Florianópolis aims to help them to do that and to plant flowers of health and happiness in their children. Since we set up the organisation in 2008, we have provided support to almost sixty families and over 200 people. Our first few families have graduated, relating improvements in child health, family income, housing, education and social inclusion. With your help, we can support more families. With your help we truly can make a difference. Thank you very much.'

I leave the microphone to the sound of enthusiastic applause. Offstage, Dr M and I battle our way out of the theatre, kissing cheeks and thanking everyone for their generously offered congratulations. We walk arm in arm across the road and down the cobblestone street. We hug warmly as we part ways and I walk onwards down the street towards my parked car.

Then something strange happens. I am suddenly swept by a wave of emotion as my childhood dream flashes vividly before me: the dream of me making the rich in Latin America aware of the needs of the poor. I feel an ebb of recognition of the similarities between the dream and my speech on the theatre stage. I am flooded with the honey-flow of a lifelong dream realised.

I hear the echo of Alastair's voice reverberate within me: 'I promise, my love, I will help you achieve all of your life goals.'

Just at that moment, I walk past an evangelical church with the double doors wide open to the street, with music blaring out. The lyrics of the music are written in huge black letters on a big white screen and the congregation sings in unison. My eyes are drawn automatically to the screen and I read the words: 'Use me Lord, Use me.' These words bring my teenage mantra immediately and forcefully to mind, 'Lord make me a handmaiden of your work.'

This stops me in my stride and I laugh out loud. I look up, look behind and look around, trying to spot the candid camera. It strikes me that I am a flute through which God is playing a sweet, sweet song.

Somehow, somewhere I have the undeniable sense that a circle is closing.

Epilogue
BREAKING UP

A couple of weeks after the awards ceremony, Alastair and my October wedding anniversary is once again approaching.

In a wave of spiritual openness and curiosity, I decide to find a way to contact Alastair and wish him a happy anniversary. A friend recommends a centre of Umbanda, an African-influenced religion widespread in Brazil, which offers the service of speaking with the spirit of a dead person manifested through a medium. My mind is full of scepticism and my cultural conditioning swamps me with finger-wagging caution, but I am learning to sidestep both of these limitations. My friend C, boyfriend W and I leave the boys with a babysitter on the night of my wedding anniversary and cross Florianópolis' bridge to the mainland. We make our way for half an hour to a long road called the Avenue of Towers, which dips and rises like a rollercoaster. In the centre of the road is an endless line of huge electricity pylons and the air outside the car buzzes with an overload of electromagnetism. Inside the car, there is a growing sense of both excitement and apprehension as we drive. We career up a steep road and arrive at the centre, cloaked in the darkness of the night.

The steps into the building are steep also and we are all panting by the time we arrive at the front door. Below us, the lights of the city shine like earthbound stars. We enter the building with the customary 'excuse me' and pass the arsenal of protection against bad spirits. There is a horseshoe at the foot of the door as we step over it and a bunch of red peppers hanging from the door handle. In a basket just inside the door, there is a pair of goat's horns. Along the corridor, there is pot after pot of protective plants: sword of St George, rue and begonia. On the wall, there is a painting of St George mounted on a horse and killing a dragon. Next to that is a poster of the local football team.

The corridor is narrow and the house is shabby. There is a pungent, sulphurous smell in the air that a young man dressed in white is trying to dispel by swinging an incense-burning thurible throughout the building. In the background, I can hear the murmur of the eight o'clock soap opera on the television. C and I swallow our misgivings, sit on a small wooden bench and wait. W stands at the door, silent and brooding as he looks down at the city lights.

There are four *filhos de santo*, or followers, in white and they move up and down the steep steps. They laugh and joke as they move. Each one wears coloured beads of red, blue, yellow, which they tell us are to invoke the protection of the gods. Each colour is for a different god. They are welcoming and kind and we chatter with them to dispel our apprehension. They seem genuine, good people who speak simply of their calling to serve at the centre. A large black woman explains to us that the spirit that manifests itself through G, the *pai de santo*, or medium, is a Belgian woman called Saba. She has been manifesting through G for over thirty years and manifested through his mother before that.

'When she was incarnated, Saba was a prostitute,' she tells us.

An older woman with dyed-blonde hair cuts her off sharply. 'No,' she says adamantly, 'she was a woman who had one man only, but he betrayed her, so she killed him.'

I breathe deeply, determined to put my rational mind aside and witness, in all openness, the effect that the energy and experience of the Umbanda Centre has on me. One of the followers calls me forward into a large ceremonial room and instructs me to take off my shoes. She explains to me that I need to light two cigarettes at a time and hand them to G, the medium.

'Saba is a chain-smoker,' she tells me.

G is standing before me. He is taller than I am and is stockily built. He looks very masculine, dressed all in black, but the way he is swaying from side to side has a grace and femininity about it. He is holding a bottle of Cachaça in his hand and swigs it at regular intervals. I light two cigarettes and hand them to him. He smokes them both simultaneously. He starts to talk and his manner is decidedly effeminate. 'You understand that I am a female spirit, speaking through this male body?' Saba asks me, swaying from side to side.

I nod my head. 'I am here to ask if you can give a message

to someone who has died,' I say, battling with my inner scepticism.

'Yes I can,' Saba informs me. 'But I can't bring anyone else to talk through the medium.'

'Can you give a message to my husband who died?' I ask and add rapidly, 'As long as it doesn't disturb him in any way.'

'What is his name?' Saba asks.

'Alastair Ramsay.'

'Was he blond?'

'No,' I answer slowly, doubting palpably, 'he had brown hair.'

The medium closes his eyes and swings from side to side. After a few minutes, Saba says, 'Ah, yes, he was met by a female family member who is buried in his home country.'

'Ah,' I say, 'I always imagined he was met by his Aunt E. She died a few years before he did and she was a second mother to him.'

The medium closes his eyes again. 'He is well, very well,' Saba tells me.

'Yes,' I say, nodding strongly, 'that is the sensation that I have.'

'He is totally clear about what happened now. He was very confused at the beginning, but now he is completely clear and understands what he did right and wrong on earth and is preparing himself to come back to another life.'

I do not know what to believe, but I wait as these words breathe peace into me.

'Will I see him again in this life?' I ask, my heart beating.

The medium's demeanour changes and he looks me straight

in the eyes and says sternly, 'No, you will not meet him again in your life. All this time, he has been watching over you and your boys, but now he is preparing for a new life. You won't cross paths with him for a very long time to come.'

'But won't he be there when I die?' I ask, nonplussed.

'No,' the medium says forcefully, taking the final drags of his two cigarettes. 'He won't be there when you die. He is not waiting for you. I am telling you that you won't live a life together again for a very long time.'

I watch how these words fall like lead in the pit of my stomach. I had not known that I had been harbouring these hopes, that I had been unconsciously holding on to him. It dawns on me that I was cradling the prospect of sitting down with him some day at some heavenly table, drinking beer and updating him on everything he missed. Reunited again, I would confide in him that I never stopped being his wife, that I never fully gave my heart to anyone else, that I was his love.

'Is– is he leaving me?' I ask, taken aback by the question as much as the feeling of adolescent vulnerability that it invokes.

The medium turns the still-lit cigarette butts into his mouth and extinguishes them with his tongue. He then flicks the cigarette butts on the floor. He stops swaying and holds on to my shoulders roughly. He looks me directly in the eyes and says emphatically, without a hint of compassion, 'Yes, he is leaving you. His story with you is over now.'

Our conversation finishes and I leave a R$50 note on a tray. I put on my shoes and stumble down the steep steps, shell-shocked. C and W follow close behind me. I am at the bottom of the stairs before I realise that I never wished Alastair a happy anniversary. Somehow, I do not think Saba would have passed on the message. For the first time since Alastair died, I feel like he has truly broken up with me. The feeling is both painful and surreal. Hadn't I accepted that we were no longer together? Hadn't these years of absence taught me he was never coming back? Even though I still feel oceans of love towards him and emanating from my memory of him, it feels like he is now fully letting go.

The next day, I go to our local video shop with the boys and they run around trying to choose a film. They start to argue about which film to pick and Liam runs off frustrated to the back of the shop. I follow after him and see that in his tantrum, he has pulled some DVD cases off a half-hidden shelf of less popular films. I bend down to pick them up and put them back on the shelf. The last of the films is lying face-up and it catches my attention. It is a low-budget 1980s film, one I would never think of renting. It is called *Always*. For some reason, I flip it around and glance at the blurb on the back. I read a part of the blurb: 'After death, a man learns to let go of his love to free her to fall in love again.' I stand up with the film in my hand and on a whim I rent it along with the boys' film, which they have now chosen. That night, after the boys have gone to bed, I watch this corny film and watch how a couple who are passionately in love are separated when the man dies suddenly. I watch how he looks over his beloved for over a year, binding her to him still. She is stuck in their story and cannot fall in love with another man or embrace life again. I cringe at the 1980s clothes and hairstyles and the questionable acting. But still I keep watching. At the end of the film, the dead man realises that the best thing he can do for his beloved is to let her go. He stands by her, unseen, and tells her with immense tenderness, 'I am moving out of your heart.' I sit there on the couch alone, sobbing the last vestiges of my loss.

That night, I dream of Alastair. We are in Ireland, in my parents' garden, and he is animatedly telling me that he was lost, but that now he has come back to me.

'But I don't want you to come back anymore,' I tell him in the dream, decidedly. 'I wanted you back for such a long time and now that you are here, I don't want you anymore.'

Even in my dream, I am shocked at my words to him and the numbness of my feelings towards him.

I awake early the next morning with an unquestionable sense of lightness. For the first time in four and a half years, I taste the gentle peace of not wanting what I do not have.

NEW LIFE

Something is missing. In the back of my mind, there is a voice telling me that life is not quite its usual self. As I rush the boys to school, it strikes me that I have not had my period for a couple of months now. I think back to the time after Alastair died and the three negative pregnancy tests I took when I did not menstruate for months. I am using the coil contraceptive, which is highly effective, so I dismiss any misgivings. A week later, my period has still not come and I buy a pregnancy test to put my mind at ease. While the boys are at school, W and I sit drinking coffee at the kitchen counter and wait for the result. 'There is nothing to worry about,' I assure W with a forced smile. 'The chances are one in three hundred.'

You would think, by now, that I would have learned not to count on probability to regulate my life. I take one more gulp of coffee and look at the white stick of the test in my hand. A definite red cross appears like magic. I laugh out loud and nearly fall off my stool. 'I was not expecting that,' I bellow disbelievingly, handing the stick to W. He guffaws nervously.

My first thought is that Alastair is reincarnating. My second thought is that this is the sister that Alastair always insisted his sons should have.

As it sinks in, this unexpected pregnancy destabilises me. The baby overcomes all odds to trumpet its arrival in our lives. Once again, I feel overwhelmed by the fact that, despite my efforts, I cannot control the major occurrences in my life. 'But I already learned that lesson,' I whine. 'Haven't I surrendered the fantasy that I have control over my life?' The pregnancy bowls me over enough to teach me that I have not yet learned this lesson well enough.

It feels initially like an involuntary wrench from the past, from the certainty and continuity of Alastair and my family of four that is crystallised in our framed photos. It catapults W and me into a commitment that neither of us has consciously made and shakes to the core our tacit agreement on a no-ties relationship. This unfettered relationship had given me the comfort of W's company, while leaving Alastair's space in the family unperturbed. This pregnancy lays to dust my projected image of the loving and loyal widow, a self-image with which I was feeling increasingly safe and secure.

Pregnancy is a blessing in its length, however. The nine months are essential not only for this baby to grow and incarnate, but also for the lessons the pregnancy brings to work their magic on me. Gradually, I come to realise that I was thinking of the pregnancy through the prism of Alastair's life rather than my own or that of this new child. The pregnancy pushes me to understand that, since his death, I have been living my life primarily through a desire to continue and fulfil Alastair's life dreams and ambitions and the dreams we shared. In the years that have passed, I have experienced many moments of acute suffering. Over time, I have shed many of the layers of suffering associated with his death. What is left is the simple, undeniable fact that I miss him. This is a kernel of pain that I accept and have learned to live with – the pain of missing this beautiful man in my life. The absence of Alastair, to paraphrase Sylvia Plath, inevitably grows beside me like a tree. There is a presence to his absence.

This suffering though, like for the oyster, has created beautiful pearls. I read once that pearls are made when sand enters the oyster, wounding its sensitive flesh. It responds intuitively by covering it with layer after layer of a substance called nacre and over time, a pearl is born. Over the years since Alastair's death, I have learned that the suffering I encounter in life, if I let it, can reward me with pearls. Pearls of gentle grace.

I now understand that the last gift Alastair gave me truly was his own death.

These years have been a beautiful and soul-reviving way of mourning and honouring Alastair and of keeping him close to me. I am filled with gratitude and humility for the gifts of love and growth Alastair showered upon me in our seven years together and through his death. This pregnancy signals to me, however, that I now have to let go, in full consciousness, of what I have been slow to relinquish. Breathing deeply and gathering together energies and courage for the future, I begin to see with a sense of clarity.

The time has now come to stop living Alastair's life through mine.

The time has now come to stop ticking off his life goals one by one.

The time has now come to accept that Alastair is no longer my 'late' husband. I no longer expect him to turn up.

In this way, I free myself to rethink my path. I free myself to live out to the full, in my own way, the rest of this one beautiful, gold-gilded life that I have been so gracefully granted.

In this way, I free myself to fully embrace new lifelong relationships that deserve their own space and attention in this changing family.

In this way too, I finally and totally free Alastair.

Alastair died at the end of May, on a Sunday morning at 4.52 a.m. My third son is born at the end of May on a Sunday morning at 4.25 a.m. Later that morning, I sit in my hospital bed with this precious beauty in my hands. My heart is overflowing with unfettered devotion. W is huddled together with my parents, recounting the details of the birth and laughing animatedly. After two Caesareans, I had managed to have a natural birth, and W and I are both exhilarated. Tom and Liam clamber up to sit at each side of me on the bed. I cradle the baby in my arms, as the two boys peer down on him in reverence.

'This is your new brother,' I tell them. 'His name is Eoin. It means "grace of God".'

The boys beam up at me and squeal with pleasure. Life, it seems, is not done with me yet.

As I hold these three life-pulsating boys to me, I congratulate myself on my beautiful family. I melt in waves of thankfulness. If for everything there truly is a season, I acknowledge with a glad and grateful heart that my time to weep and mourn has passed and now is my time to laugh and dance.

Acknowledgements

Writing this book is the fulfilment of a life dream of mine and of my husband, Alastair James Ramsay, who died suddenly in 2007. On a list of dreams that Alastair wrote down a couple of years before he died, one was to have his name on the front cover of a book. With this book, therefore, I tick off the last of his dreams that I can directly help him to realise. It is also the fulfilment of my aspiration as a writer. Alastair often used to say that I should write a book. During the year before he died, he stated knowingly, 'Something dramatic has to happen to you, to push you into writing your book.' Alastair's own sudden death was the dramatic event that resulted in this, my first book. Once again, I hear the whisper of his voice, 'I promise, my love, I will help you achieve all of your life goals.'

I am deeply grateful for all of the support that was lavished on me and the boys after Alastair's death. I am very rich in family and friends and I thank God for them. My mother-in-law Pam and sister-in-law Nikki were among the most generous in this support, especially at times that were particularly painful for them. I melt in gratitude to Byron Katie, Osho and Swaha for cradling me in my loss and for giving me tools to come to an acceptance of Alastair's death and initiate a more authentic approach to life. I also thank my other masters, my three sons: Tom, who kept the past alive; Liam, who brought me back to the present; and Eoin, who opened me up to the future.

Thank you to those who pushed me to write this book, suggested improvements and encouraged me to share it. It is impossible to name everyone, but I am conscious and grateful for the support of each one of you. I will name just the person who started me off and the person who finished the process. Sally J, Alastair's great friend, suggested that I write a blog while I was in Brazil as a starting point for writing a book. This was exactly the spur I needed – thank you, Sally! Livy L, my great friend, rang me on my mobile phone in Brazil after reading the first draft of the book and told me to leave it to her to get it published. A couple of weeks later, we were talking to Hachette. Livy, as a good friend of ours would say, you're awesome!

Thank you to Ciara and the team at Hachette for the sensitive editing and for believing in the book.

Finally, no mother of three young children writes and edits a book without alot of help. Thank you Walbert, Cida, Alex, Marisa, Dani, Gitali and Marcelo for minding the kids.

Writing this book has been a healing journey. Thank you for sharing it with me.

Resources that I found most helpful

- www.thework.com
- Byron Katie, *A Thousand Names for Joy – Living in Harmony With the Ways Things Are*
- Osho, *Learning to Silence the Mind and Dynamic Meditations*, www.oshointernational.com
- www.vasantswaha.net
- Joan Didion, *The Year of Magical Thinking*
- C. S. Lewis, *A Grief Observed*
- Natascha McElhone, *After You*
- Rabbi Harold Kushner, *When Bad Things Happen to Good People*
- Elisabeth Kübler Ross, *On Death and Dying*
- Sogyal Rinpoche, *The Tibetan Book of Living and Dying*
- Dr. Sam Parnia, *What Happens When We Die? A Groundbreaking Study into the Nature of Life and Death*
- *Gifts of Grief* documentary, www.giftsofgrief.com
- *Always*, DVD of the 1989 movie

Permission Acknowledgements

'Fairytale Of New York'. Words & Music by Shane MacGowan & Jem Finer. © Copyright 1987 Universal Music Publishing Limited/ Universal Music Publishing MGB Limited. All Rights Reserved. International Copyright Secured. Used by permission of Music Sales Limited.

'Do Not Go Gentle Into That Good Night', taken from *The Poems* by Dylan Thomas, published by Orion Publishing Group. Used by permission of David Higham Associates Limited.

'The Blower's Daughter'. Words & Music by Damien George Rice. © Copyright 2003 Warner/Chappell Music Publishing Ltd (PRS). All Rights Reserved.

The Prophet (1923) by Kahlil Gibran. Published in 2011 by William Heinemann Ltd, part of Cornerstone Publishing.

'Aedh Wishes for the Cloths of Heaven', taken from *The Wind Among the Reeds* (1899) by William Butler Yeats.

'Gratitude to the Unknown Instructors', taken from *The Winding Stair* (1933) by William Butler Yeats.

'Satyricon' by Petronius (quoted in the preface to 'The Waste Land' by T. S. Eliot). Originally published in the first century AD.

'Death is nothing at all' by Henry Scott Holland.

The publisher has endeavoured to contact all copyright holders of material featured within the book. We apologise for any omissions and encourage copyright holders of any material not credited to make contact on info@hbgi.ie.